Search for a National Retirement Income Policy

Other publications of the
PENSION RESEARCH COUNCIL:

Fundamentals of Private Pensions—*Dan M. McGill*
Concepts of Actuarial Soundness in Pension Plans—*Dorrance C. Bronson*
Social Aspects of Retirement—*Otto Pollak*
Positive Experiences in Retirement—*Otto Pollak*
Ensuring Medical Care for the Aged—*Mortimer Spiegelman*
Legal Protection of Private Pension Expectations—*Edwin W. Patterson*
Legal Status of Employee Benefit Rights under Private Pension Plans—*Benjamin Aaron*
Decision and Influence Processes in Private Pension Plans—*James E. McNulty, Jr.*
Fulfilling Pension Expectations—*Dan M. McGill*
Collectively Bargained Multi-Employer Pension Plans—*Joseph J. Melone*
Actuarial Aspects of Pension Security—*William F. Marples*
Status of Funding under Private Pension Plans—*Frank L. Griffin, Jr.* and *Charles L. Trowbridge* (out of print)
Guaranty Fund for Private Pension Obligations—*Dan M. McGill*
Preservation of Pension Benefit Rights—*Dan M. McGill*
Retirement Systems for Public Employees—*Thomas P. Bleakney*
Employer Guarantee of Pension Benefits—*Dan M. McGill*
Reciprocity among Private Multiemployer Pension Plans—*Maurice E. McDonald*
A New Look at Accounting for Pension Costs—*William D. Hall* and *David L. Landsittel*
Social Security and Private Pension Plans: Competitive or Complementary?—*Dan M. McGill* (ed.)
Pension Mathematics—*Howard E. Winklevoss*
Indexation of Pension and Other Benefits—*Robert J. Meyers*
Joint Trust Pension Plans—*Daniel F. McGinn*
Financing the Civil Service Retirement System—*Dan M. McGill* (ed.)
Continuing Care Retirement Communities—*Howard E. Winklevoss* and *Alwyn V. Powell*
Social Investing—*Dan M. McGill* (ed.)
Employer Accounting for Pensions—*E. L. Hicks* and *C. L. Trowbridge*
Pensions, Economics and Public Policy—*Richard A. Ippolito*

Search for a National Retirement Income Policy

Edited by
Jack L. VanDerhei
Associate Research Director
Pension Research Council

1987

Published for the
Pension Research Council
Wharton School
University of Pennsylvania
by

RICHARD D. IRWIN, INC.
Homewood, Illinois 60430

ISBN 0-256-05606-4

Library of Congress Catalog Card No. 86-71610

Printed in the United States of America

1 2 3 4 5 6 7 8 9 0 MP 4 3 2 1 0 9 8 7

Pension Research Council

PURPOSE OF THE COUNCIL

The Pension Research Council was formed in 1952 to undertake academic research into those institutional arrangements designed to provide financial resources for secure and dignified old age. It seeks to broaden public understanding of these complex arrangements through basic research into their social, economic, legal, actuarial, and financial foundations. While generally geared to the long view of the pension institution, projects undertaken by the Council are always relevant to real life concerns and frequently focus on issues under current debate. The Council does not speak with one voice and espouses no particular point of view. The members do share a general desire to encourage and strengthen private-sector approaches to old-age economic security, while recognizing the essential role of Social Security and other income-maintenance programs in the public sector.

This volume is a collection of papers presented at the 1985 Economic Security Symposium, cosponsored by the Pension Research Council and the Boettner Research Institute of the American College, held November 6–7, 1985, on the Bryn Mawr, Pennsylvania, campus of the college. The purpose of the symposium was to bring together on an invitational basis persons from business, labor, government, and academia to address the financial questions of a national retirement income policy.

The Boettner Research Institute is committed to the advancement of knowledge about economic well-being and its relationship to psychological and physical well-being of persons in our maturing and aging society.

This book is being published by funds from the Ralph H. Blanchard Endowment of the Pension Research Council. Mr. Blanchard was one of the founders of an organization now known as Mutual Life Insurance Company of America.

Preface

The various methods of providing economic security for the retired population have often been likened to a three-legged stool—supported by individual efforts, group efforts (usually in the form of employer-sponsored benefits), and government programs. Estimates based on recent figures prepared by the staff of the Joint Committee on Taxation using information from the IRS Statistics of Income and the 1984 Current Population Survey indicate that Social Security benefits are received by over 90 percent of taxpayers 65 and older and represent 29 percent of their total income. Approximately 18 percent of the total income is attributed to pension income; however, 52 percent of the returns included at least some pension income. The average amount obtained from all sources for this group was slightly less than $20,000 per return.[1]

In recent years there have been a number of forces influencing retirement policy in this country. Perhaps the most important catalyst for change in this area has been the constant modification in the tax law. Three major laws enacted in the last five years have had substantial impact on the incentives to use certain individual and group savings mechanisms. The Economic Recovery Tax Act of 1981 (ERTA) introduced several retirement-related tax breaks. Deductions for Individual Retirement Arrangements (IRAs) were increased from $1,500 to $2,000 with a similar $500 increase in spousal accounts. More important, the eligibility requirements for IRAs were liberalized to include active participants in employer-sponsored retirement plans. Rules for Simplified Employee Pensions (SEPs) and Keogh plans were also changed, including a doubling of the maximum contributions to $15,000.

In 1982, the Tax Equity and Fiscal Responsibility Act (TEFRA) substantially cut back many of the incentives to provide for economic security through employer-sponsored benefits. Limitations on contributions and benefits from qualified

[1]Joint Committee on Taxation, *Tax Reform Proposals: Pensions and Deferred Compensation* (JCS-33-85), August 5, 1985, pp. 3–4.

retirement plans were reduced by one third and a "temporary" freeze imposed on cost-of-living adjustments to these limits. On the other hand, the tax consequences of plans loans were modified in a way that increased the incentives to use the plan for retirement purposes. The most drastic effects of this law have probably resulted from the addition of top-heavy plan provisions to the tax code. With many small pension plans forced into faster vesting schedules, lower compensation ceilings, more restrictive integration formulas, and increased benefits to nonkey employees, the incentives to continue to use this form of plan to provide retirement income have been diminished.

The effects of TEFRA, however, were not restricted solely to the group approach. Deferred annuity contracts with insurance companies, which had become an increasingly important form of individual savings, were subjected to a less advantageous form of taxation in the case of early payouts. Moreover, new tests were introduced for universal life insurance policies that substantially limited the maximum investment component available.

The Deficit Reduction Act of 1984 (DEFRA) contained several provisions that substantially modified savings incentives. Cost-of-living adjustments for contributions and benefit limits were frozen for a second time. Estate tax exclusions for distributions from qualified plans and IRAs were repealed. Rules for cash-or-deferred plans [aka, 401(k) plans] were tightened. DEFRA may have an additional impact on economic security for the retired population due to decreased incentives for employers to continue group medical benefits past the employee's retirement age. Employers have lost significant tax advantages on contributions to, and income from, reserves established to fund retirees' medical benefits, whether held in a welfare plan or by an insurance company.

Social Security, the other leg of the economic security stool for retirees, has not been immune from congressional action either. The Social Security Amendments Act of 1983 subjected benefits to taxation in some situations, delayed the normal retirement age for future generations of retirees, and gave workers increased incentive to defer retirement.

During this continuing evolution of changes in the forces influencing pension policy there has often been a call for a concentrated effort to develop some type of national retirement income policy. It was in this environment that the 1985 Economic Security Symposium was developed. The symposium, cosponsored by the Pension Research Council of the Wharton School and the Boettner Research Institute of the American College, was held in Bryn Mawr, Pennsylvania, on November 6–7, 1985. The purpose of the symposium was to bring together on an invitational basis persons from business, labor, government, and academia to address the fundamental questions of a national retirement income policy. This permitted the role of the key players in this process to be examined by a select group of program participants and allowed public policy considerations to be analyzed by those people directly involved in making decisions in Washington at this critical time.

This volume is made up of papers presented at the symposium. The first chapter of the book deals primarily with the federal income tax considerations involved in a national retirement income policy. Senator Bill Bradley, coauthor of the Bradley-Gephardt tax reform proposal, describes the evolution of the three-legged stool for retirement income in the United States and examines the existing tax system with a view to the dual objective of ensuring that (1) retirement income security is available to all who have worked, and (2) tax policy in this area is truly fair.

The next chapter provides a broad perspective of the principal means of assuring that the material needs of the retired population are met. Professor Dan M. McGill, Chairman of the Pension Research Council and the Wharton School's Insurance Department, provides a conceptual analysis of the evolution of governmental and employer-sponsored retirement programs and the public policy issues these programs currently present. He also discusses the responsiveness of personal savings to tax incentives and highlights the major policy decisions that need to be made in the near future.

The third chapter, written by Peter K. Francese, editor of *American Demographics*, provides a background for the discussion of economic security in retirement with his description of our multidimensional population. He discusses three demographic dimensions of the elderly that have an impact on their economic security: age distribution, income characteristics, and family structure.

In Chapter 4, Richard A. Ippolito, Director of Research, Pension Program, U.S. Department of Labor, evaluates government policy toward retirement income. Based on the assumption that the goal of government policy is to engender the effective allocation of resources, Dr. Ippolito concentrates his analysis on the most important elements of national retirement income policy: Social Security, pension taxation, pension regulation, and pension insurance. He proceeds to determine which government policies are consistent with the national policy and recommends changes in public laws that fall outside its bounds.

In Chapter 5, Professor C. Arthur Williams, Jr., of the University of Minnesota traces the history of Social Security and examines the basic principles on which it has been based. Dr. Williams describes some of the revolutionary and evolutionary changes that have been proposed for the future of the system.

In Chapter 6, William F. May, Chairman of the Committee for Economic Development's Research and Policy Committee and former Chairman of American Can, presents a perspective from the business world on future policies for employer-based pension plans. He outlines several ideas and proposals to redirect the debate on pension issues.

In the next chapter, Robert D. Paul, Vice Chairman of Martin E. Segal, outlines the issues of economic security from the employee's perspective. He discusses the historical evolution of employer and government responsibility for economic security in the United States, points out the concerns of the current era in the employee benefits field, and offers his prospects for the future.

The role of the pension industry in implementing a national retirement income policy is described in Chapter 8. This chapter was prepared by George B. Swick, retired chairman of George B. Buck Consulting Actuaries, Inc. Before retiring, Mr. Swick had accumulated more than 30 years of consulting experience with the Buck firm. In his paper, he draws from his vast experience in the industry to provide an analysis of the evolving trends and future prospects for the leading players in this industry and the role they serve in the overall system.

The final chapter of the book addresses the issue of tax policy for retirement income. Written by Daniel I. Halperin, Professor of Law at Georgetown University Law Center, the chapter focuses on two important policy issues: (1) why particular employees may not be entitled to receive benefits when they retire, even though the company they work for has a plan in force, and (2) what should be done for employees who are entitled to retirement benefits but do not receive enough to replace preretirement income. The questions of whether voluntary employer plans can be modified to produce coverage that is considered adequate and whether alternative approaches to retirement security are viable are also discussed.

The only session not represented in this volume was a panel discussion on individual action for economic security. Joseph J. Melone, President of the Prudential Insurance Company of America, moderated this session. The panelists, Kathleen Utgoff, Executive Director of the Pension Benefit Guaranty Corporation; C. Arthur Williams; and Robert Paul, discussed several important issues ranging from international competition and macroeconomic policy to the appropriate qualification requirements for 401(k) plans.

The editor expresses his deep appreciation to the authors of the various papers in this volume. The many people whose advice and assistance have contributed greatly to this volume include the codirectors of the symposium, Drs. Dan M. McGill and Davis W. Gregg, Boettner Distinguished Professor, The American College; Yung-Ping Chen, Frank M. Engle Professor in Economic Security Research, the American College; Mildred A. Brill, Business Administrator, the Pension Research Council; and the coordinator of the symposium, Helen L. Schmidt, Research Associate, Boettner Research Institute, the American College.

Any opinions expressed in this volume are those of the respective authors and do not reflect the view of the Pension Research Council, its individual members, or any of the sponsoring organizations.

Jack L. VanDerhei

Contents

1 Economic Security in Retirement: Whose Responsibility?

by The Honorable Bill Bradley*

In this country, the whole notion of planning for retirement is a relatively recent phenomenon. A century ago, when life expectancy was 46 years, most men worked until they died, and most men and women who couldn't work were supported by their families.

But times have changed. Life expectancy has increased dramatically. People aged 65 can now expect to live an additional 10 to 20 years. And since people are living longer, they are spending a smaller portion of their life span in the labor force. A man born in 1900 spent about 70 percent of his life in the labor force; a man born today will only spend a little more than half of his life in the labor force.

That adds up to fewer years of income production and more years of nonproduction. Hence, the need for more retirement planning.

Since the 1930s, experts have come to view retirement income as a three-legged stool made up of Social Security, private pensions, and savings. This system has served us fairly well. In 1950, when only one out of four elderly persons received Social Security and very few people received pensions, over 35 per-

*U.S. Senator (Democrat), New Jersey.

cent of the elderly were living in poverty. Currently, with 9 out of 10 elderly persons receiving Social Security and one quarter of retirees receiving pensions, only 14 percent of older Americans fall below the poverty line. It is fair to conclude that our three-legged stool has generally succeeded in providing adequate economic security for the elderly.

But the changing nature and needs of our elderly require that we broaden our definition of "adequate economic security." What was considered adequate 30 years ago is certainly not adequate today. And what is adequate today won't be adequate in 30 years.

Today's retirees and those who approach retirement are not just concerned about how to pay the rent and buy food. Another economic need overwhelms those relatively small monetary requirements. The need for long-term health care is apparent, and its astronomical cost frightens them.

The greatest economic risk that the elderly currently face is the risk of incurring massive health-care costs. And this risk will grow over time. To the extent that our current three-legged stool fails to take into account these increased costs, our system will fail to meet the economic security needs of retirees.

Given this expanded view of economic security in retirement, how will our three-legged stool hold up as our nation ages? Which legs will need to be strengthened to ensure economic security? And who will have to take more responsibility for ensuring economic security in retirement—we as individuals, we as employers, or we as a nation?

These are not simple questions. Our European friends are currently grappling with the issue of how to provide adequate economic security to their rapidly growing aging population. And one thing is certain: We won't be far behind them—especially when the baby boom of 1950 becomes the senior boom in the early part of the next century.

So, what does the future hold for our three-legged stool?

Social Security

It is impossible to discuss U.S. retirement policy without starting with the Social Security Act, one of this nation's most significant achievements. It would not be an exaggeration to say that Social Security wrought major changes in the fabric of American life. Passage of this legislation in 1935 represented the expression of a new, emerging, and growing consensus—a consensus that we as individuals are not islands—that we have responsibilities for the well-being of our neighbors as well as of ourselves. As this consensus developed, the first tentative safety net in America took shape.

Fifty years ago, when the question was asked, "Who is responsible for retirement security?" the answer was clear: individuals and their families. When the question is asked today, most Americans answer that we as a nation are also partly responsible. Social Security is how this responsibility is discharged: Those who are able to be productive—the young and employed—provide to those who are not—the elderly and disabled.

A recent public opinion poll concluded that extremely strong support exists among all age groups for the continuation of the Social Security program. Roughly 9 out of 10 Americans oppose the phasing out of Social Security and replacing it with reliance on private pension plans. Three quarters of all Americans consider the Social Security tax to be fair (compare that to the income tax), and only one quarter of Americans think that the Social Security tax is too high.

This sense of community and commitment was readily apparent in 1982, when it was becoming increasingly clear that the Social Security Trust Fund was in imminent danger of insolvency; corrective measures had to be adopted or the July 1, 1983, Social Security check would not be in the mail. The legislation that was adopted asked everyone to pitch in to save the system. And everyone did, because everyone saw the need to pitch in to keep this important life-support system going. The legislative changes adopted in 1983 put the Social Security retirement program on sound footing for several decades. And the progressive benefit structure, coupled with taxation of benefits, will ensure that an increasing share of benefits will go to lower-income elderly.

Over the next 25 years, I don't anticipate major changes in the retirement component of Social Security; I foresee a mature retirement system with a stable benefit structure that continues to replace the current levels of preretirement income as well as a stable tax system to finance this level of benefits.

But when we look at the Medicare Trust Fund, another essential component of our retirement security policy, we see a very different situation. Under most economic forecasts, Medicare Trust Fund reserves will be depleted well before the first Baby Boomer nears retirement. Strong cost containment measures will have to be instituted if we are to live up to our current commitments to provide minimally adequate acute-care coverage. And this doesn't take into account the growing costs associated with the long-term care needs of the elderly.

Somewhere in our three-legged stool, we will have to find the means to finance these rapidly increasing costs. Where is the money going to come from? Will the retirement and health-care components of Social Security be able to pick up all or part of these costs?

Short of increasing Social Security revenues, there is one pot of money that could be available over the next couple of decades for expanded benefits. According to the Social Security actuaries, the Retirement Trust Fund is scheduled to build up massive surpluses—$7 trillion over the next 30 years. There will be suggestions that we use those funds to expand Medicare benefits or expand cash benefits to help the elderly pay for increased health-care costs. But if we do that we will not have the funds needed in the period 2015 to 2040 to pay basic Social Security retirement benefits to the baby-boom generation. If the Congress spends the surplus on expanded benefits, rather than saving it for the senior-boom generation, the Social Security system will be in a very, very precarious condition in 30 years: tax rates will have to skyrocket to pay retirement benefits. Clearly, then, we would pay a big price for failing to find a way in the near future to finance these health-care costs.

In sum, in the years ahead, the Social Security retirement benefit will continue to be the largest single source of income for most elderly Americans, with an increasing share of benefits targeted to lower-income elderly. The program should be able to replace roughly the same proportion of preretirement income as it currently does. But the economic needs of the elderly, as individuals and as a group, will increase in future years. Will we be able to significantly expand benefits beyond their current levels to cover these additional costs? Will Social Security be able to become a considerably larger leg of our stool? I think not. Therefore, most of the increases in retirement income will have to come from the private legs of the stool—savings and pensions.

The Other Legs of the Stool

The elderly's asset and pension income has been growing in recent years. Savings amounted to 23 percent of the elderly's total income in 1981, up from 15 percent in 1967. And about 14 percent of the elderly's income comes from pensions, up from 9 percent in 1962.

As of 1983, about 50 percent of all private industry employees 18 years old and older were covered by pensions in their current jobs. Although some growth will occur, that percentage is expected to be relatively stable for the foreseeable future. If past behavior continues, about half of the covered workers (one-fourth of all workers) can expect to receive pensions when they reach retirement age.

Pensions will continue to be an important retirement security component. But unless we can increase the number of employees getting pensions, this component will not provide extra security for a considerable share of the population.

What is the outlook for savings? The Baby Boomers have not been in a position up until now to save much or to vest in pensions. But the next 20 to 30 years may be different. Right now, the Baby Boomers are settling down, buying houses and consumer goods, and settling into careers. We may see a real increase in the savings rate for this age group as they start to prepare for retirement. This would be a very favorable outcome. We need to do whatever we can to encourage savings.

The Role of Tax Policy

Under the federal income tax system, people are generally taxed on income as it is earned. Historically, exceptions to this rule have been made to encourage certain retirement savings.

Present tax law provides incentives by permitting taxpayers to postpone income tax on current compensation set aside for retirement and on the investment earnings of those savings, under special pension and deferred-compensation plans.

There have been two reasons for granting favorable treatment to these retirement plans: first, to encourage individuals to save for their own retirement and, second, to create additional savings that contribute to the formation of investment capital needed for economic growth.

While many people criticize tax policy for not doing enough to encourage people to save more, others identify serious shortcomings in the current approach. For example, there is concern that tax-preferred retirement savings provide disproportionately generous benefits to the relatively well-off while neglecting the neediest Americans. We can gauge whether this concern is justified by looking at the primary sources of income among persons of retirement age. These include wages and salaries, pensions, Social Security benefits, interest and dividends, and capital gains. According to a recent study by the Congress' Committee on Taxation, Social Security benefits plus distributions from pension plans comprise less than half of all income going to taxpayers over 65.[1] Social Security benefits represent the largest single source of income to these taxpayers. But while over 90 percent of the elderly received at least some Social Security benefits, those benefits represented less than 30 percent of total income from all sources ($113 billion of $387 billion in 1983). An amount almost as large, $103 billion, came from interest and dividends.

Of the total $387 billion in total income received by those over 65, only about 18 percent ($70 billion) came from public and private pensions.

These statistics raise important equity issues. Relatively few taxpayers aged 65 and over benefit from tax-preferred pension and other retirement plans. Yet everyone—including the elderly—subsidizes these plans by paying higher tax rates on income that does not enjoy special treatment, like interest and dividends. For the period fiscal years 1986–90, the revenue loss

---

[1]*Editor's note:* For the results of this study, see Joint Committee on Taxation, *Tax Reform Proposals: Pensions and Deferred Compensation* (JCS-33-85), August 5, 1985, p. 4.

attributable to the various tax-favored income security provisions is projected to reach almost $450 billion. We make up for this loss by higher tax rates on income that does not get favored treatment and on which most retired people depend.

While I am not advocating repeal of all the tax preferences currently available to retirement income, I do believe we need to examine the existing system with a view to ensuring that retirement income security is available to everyone who has worked and earned and that our tax policy in this area is truly fair.

We also need to take a hard look at whether the present tax law achieves the second rationale for tax-preferred retirement vehicles, namely, encouraging more savings. Here, the record is clouded at best. Let us take a look at Individual Retirement Arrangements (IRA) as a case in point. Available data show, not surprisingly, that the greatest participation is among middle- and upper-income taxpayers. In 1983, over 66 percent of total IRA contributions were made by taxpayers with adjusted gross income over $30,000. In addition, this group was responsible for over 75 percent of total spousal IRA contributions.

These data have led many to argue that such tax-preferred savings vehicles result in greater retirement income only for taxpayers whose savings are more than likely to be adequate during retirement, even without a tax break. Thus, the incentives merely shift part of the cost of this group's retirement savings to the federal government, which in turn shifts that cost to taxpayers as a whole in the form of higher tax rates.

In addition, studies show that IRA contributions have not come from new savings—notwithstanding Congress' expectation when it adopted the IRA provisions that this would happen. Most experts agree that there is no evidence of any change in the U.S. savings rate looked at from a historical perspective, and, if anything, the most recent data suggest saving is on the decline. And there is a growing consensus, reflected in all the pending tax reform proposals, that the existing incentives simply have not worked. Not only have they not increased savings, they have also reduced the progressivity of the tax laws and introduced serious distortions into the allocation of capital.

It may be that saving simply is not very responsive to tax changes that increase after-tax rewards. But even if it is, the existing incentives are, for the most part, not well designed to achieve their stated goals. For one thing, most of the savings tax benefits go to taxpayers who merely switch assets from one form of saving (or one kind of account) to another. Taking money out of one's savings account to put into an IRA will reduce your taxes but it does nothing to increase savings.

Another shortcoming is that the tax code still rewards borrowing. Thus, a taxpayer can borrow and deduct the interest to purchase an asset whose income is fully or partially tax exempt. This gives him a tax reduction even though his net saving has not increased. This problem, I should add, is exacerbated by inflation because the deduction for nominal interest payments may result in a negative real after-tax borrowing rate.

So if we are serious about legislating tax incentives that will really encourage saving, as opposed to tax arbitrage, we need to pay much greater attention to designing incentives that work. And we need to get rid of the tax provisions that encourage borrowing.

And if we are serious about promoting pension savings as a way of enhancing both capital formation and retirement security, we might want to take a hard look at what all those funds are being used for. I am especially troubled, as I know many others are, by recent corporate attempts to divert billions in surplus pension money to other uses, such as takeover financing. Indeed, the mergers and acquisitions craze of the last two years appears to owe much of its vitality to pension fund redemptions. For example, the Occidental Petroleum Corporation financed part of its Cities Service purchase with $400 million from Cities' pension plans; Mobil captured $29 million in excess pension funds after it took over Superior Oil; and the St. Regis Corporation collected $88 million after the acquisition of Champion International's assets. Even the administration has recognized there is a problem here. To deal with it, a 10 percent excise tax on all profits from pension funds redemptions has been proposed. With pension assets of well over a trillion dollars, it is appropriate for government to worry about just how those assets are deployed and for whose benefit.

In my judgment, the single most effective tax policy for achieving these goals is to lower tax rates and broaden the tax base. Few would question that there is a public purpose in giving an incentive for a pension to provide an adequate, indeed a comfortable, retirement. But beyond a certain level, individuals should save for themselves out of after-tax dollars. This is particularly true under a tax reform measure like the Bradley-Gephardt Fair Tax, where 80 percent of taxpayers pay no more than 14 percent in tax and the highest rate on any income is 30 percent. That is a powerful incentive for saving for retirement, or indeed for any other purpose.

Moreover, lowering the tax rates and broadening the base would ensure that income is taxed more uniformly, thereby improving resource allocation and directing capital toward the most efficient—not merely the most tax-preferred—uses. Lower rates would reinforce this positive effect. It would also promote savings by reducing the tax subsidy for borrowing. Finally, because tax preferences really redistribute a greater share of the total tax burden to those who are not rich enough or sophisticated enough to take advantage of complex tax rules, a low-rate broad-based tax would significantly enhance tax fairness.

U.S. Retirement Policy and the International Economy

A recent development is the contribution of all federal expenditures and transfers to a federal budget deficit that is sending shock waves through the international economy. In order to finance this budget deficit, U.S. interest rates have risen and attracted a massive inflow of capital from abroad. This capital inflow, on the order of $100 billion per year, helps to raise the value of the dollar on international currency markets and thus perpetuates the trade deficit that is eroding U.S. manufacturing competitiveness.

If Americans were saving at a considerably higher rate, these international problems would be minimized, because we wouldn't need major inflows of foreign capital to finance our deficit.

Social Security plays a special role among the categories of government expenditure contributing indirectly to the U.S. trade deficit. This is because Social Security—as important and beneficial as it is—also tends to discourage U.S. savings. It is not necessary to save as much for retirement to the extent that Social Security provides retirement income that is protected against inflation. Between 1965 and 1983 Social Security and SSI coverage increased from 82 percent to 96 percent of the over-65 population, while personal savings dropped from 7.1 percent to 5 percent of disposable income.

Decreased U.S. savings forces the government to borrow from abroad. Borrowing from Japanese savers has been particularly large, amounting to an estimated $35 billion to $40 billion in 1984. Government borrowing from abroad is an immediate cause of the U.S. trade deficit, since it drains the dollars that foreigners would otherwise spend on U.S. exports.

In sum, we are faced with the possibility that the government's leg of the retirement stool is inadvertently contributing to some extent to the erosion of U.S. industrial competitiveness. Social Security discourages U.S. savings, and maybe that's the price of humane government, but it forces the government to borrow from abroad. This borrowing cuts into our export markets. In a very real sense, because of our large deficits, U.S. industry and Social Security beneficiaries are competing for foreign resources, and until we can revitalize U.S. savings rates, or cut the budget deficit, U.S. industry will continue to lose ground.

That does not mean that we end or even reduce our support for Social Security. What it does mean is that until we get our deficits down to manageable size, there will be a tension between meeting the needs of the elderly and economic growth.

Summary

In summary, as we age as a nation, our definition of retirement security will have to expand. The elderly—as individuals and as a group—are going to need more than our current commitments will provide. Their expanded needs will have to be met. The remaining chapters in this book will examine how we do that.

Failure to satisfactorily meet the challenge may well create a tension between meeting the needs of the elderly and other responsibilities of families and of government. That is a tension that need not be significant if we take effective action to plan for the long-term health needs of the elderly, if we reform our income tax system to encourage private savings through overall reduction of rates, and if we move more effectively than we have to get our budget deficits under control.

How well we accomplish those tasks will determine not only the welfare of our elderly but the economic welfare of our country.

2 Broad Perspectives

by Dan M. McGill*

Every generation requires a strategy for its collective old age. An example of one strategy and its potential consequences is found in a folktale that has been recited throughout Europe since the 13th century.[1] It is the story of an old merchant who day by day grows more infirm. The old man's wife has long since passed away, and he is miserably lonely. Out of loneliness and fear that he will soon be unable to care for himself, he asks his middle-aged son and daughter-in-law if he might move into their spacious home in the country.

The couple's reluctance to permit this intrusion into their family life is overcome by the old man's promise to bequeath his small fortune to them by way of compensation. But in his dotage the old man becomes increasingly difficult to care for. The daughter-in-law becomes resentful of his needs and his senile chatter. Indeed, she harangues her husband night and day until he sorrowfully agrees that the time has come to put the old man in the barn.

---

*Chairman, Pension Research Council, and Professor of Insurance, Wharton School.

[1]Adapted from "The Tale of the Ungrateful Son," in Phillip Longman, "Justice between Generations," *Atlantic*, June 1985, p. 73.

The son is too embarrassed to confront his father directly with his shameful decision. He gives that unpleasant task to his youngest child.

"Take your grandfather to the barn and wrap him in the best horse blanket we have on the farm," he tells the boy. "That way the old man will be as comfortable as possible until he dies."

With tears in his eyes the child does as he is told, except that, having selected the farm's best horse blanket, he tears it in half. He uses one part to swaddle his beloved grandfather but sets the other part aside. The merchant's son is furious when he learns what his child has done. "What sort of boy are you who would put his own grandfather out in the barn to freeze with only half a horse blanket?" he shouts.

"But father," the child replies. "I am saving the other half for you."

Of all the living things on earth, mankind is the only species that manifests any real concern for the less fortunate members of its universe, especially those too old to fend for themselves. If an antelope on the plains develops a limp, it is only a matter of hours until it becomes another animal's meal. If a bird in the wild breaks a wing, it will not live to raise its young or build another nest. Even the lordly lion, when it grows too old and weak to hunt, winds up as the uncooked filet mignon of the stalking jackal and other scavengers.

In human society, there are different customs and attitudes toward proper treatment of superannuated members. Until recent times Eskimos who felt that they had become a burden to their families were expected to walk out of their igloos and trudge along the icy tundras until they froze to death. As recently as 20 years ago, the native Indian tribes on an island off the shores of Costa Rica had the quaint custom of throwing a farewell party for a member no longer able to carry his own weight, after which the honored individual was rowed out in a boat and tossed into the open sea. Closer to home and within the last year, the governor of a prominent western state has asserted that terminally ill old people have an obligation to die!

Despite these aberrations from the norm, civilized societies throughout the world recognize and accept a responsibility for meeting the essential needs of the members of those societies, especially those whose productive days are past. There are, of course, differences among societies as to the evaluation of the needs and the means adopted to meet them.

In today's environment, the principal means of assuring that the material needs of the general population are met are governmentally sponsored programs, employer-sponsored programs, and individual savings.

Governmentally Sponsored Programs

The Elizabethan Poor Laws, enacted by Parliament in 1601, are generally regarded to be the first systematic, governmental approach to dealing with poverty in all its manifestations. While the approach may have been a vast improvement over anything that preceded it, it was far from a benevolent one. Over the years the laws were amended to reflect the general perception that the indigent were poor because, in essence, they were a lazy lot of worthless loafers. It became a matter of public policy that an indigent be made to earn his keep, regardless of his affliction or physical condition. That policy was implemented through the establishment of workhouses, which became sources of cheap labor—some say convict labor—for local entrepreneurs.

This harsh system of public assistance was adopted, almost to the letter, in colonial America, beginning with the Massachusetts Bay Colony in 1639. It continued throughout the 18th and 19th centuries, mitigated only by the assistance provided by craft guilds, benevolent societies, and union-sponsored pension and welfare plans. In the latter half of the 19th century, many countries came to the realization that national income-maintenance programs were needed to deal with the general problem of dependency, especially that associated with old age. Beginning with Germany, one European country after the other set up a national compulsory old-age insurance system. It was not until 1935, however, that the U.S. Congress recognized the inadequacy of existing private and public efforts to deal with old-age economic dependency in the United States and passed the Social Security Act.

Today in all developed countries the foundation of the old-age economic security structure is a national compulsory, universal old-age insurance program. While differing in details, these programs have the common purpose of assuring the covered population a minimum level of income, payable as a right and not as a means-tested gratuity. What constitutes a minimum level of support has been a subject of debate over the years and continues to generate considerable controversy. The controversy in the United States is not so much on the question of whether Social Security benefits are *adequate* as on the issue of whether they are more than adequate or even *excessive*. Clarity of thinking on the subject is not encouraged by the vagueness of the language used to articulate the goal of Social Security. The goal is variously expressed as "keeping persons off the relief rolls," "providing a standard of health and decency," "minimum subsistence," and "floor of protection." For years the Social Security Administration had an unofficial quantitative measure of the adequacy of old-age *insurance* benefits. It was assumed, as a rough operating guide, that such benefits had been pitched at a sufficiently high level if no more than 10 percent of benefit recipients needed to have their income supplemented by old-age *assistance*, a national program providing means-tested benefits (now called Supplemental Security Income). There was no objective test as to whether the insurance benefit level was too high.

Over the years a term that has gained general acceptance as an expression of the *minimum* benefits goal is *social adequacy*. In a national old-age insurance program providing flat benefits (demogrants) financed from general revenues, the principal policy question is whether the benefits are too small, too large, or just right. When benefits are wage related, however, and the program is financed by payroll taxes levied on both employers and employees, "equity" concerns are introduced into the equation. The question is raised as to whether there should be an actuarial equivalence between the payroll taxes paid by and on behalf of a given individual (or discrete group of individuals) and the value of the protection and benefits made available to that individual.

Some groups argue that since the program is compulsory, there is a moral obligation to operate the program along traditional insurance lines and maintain a rough equivalence between taxes paid by or on behalf of a particular individual and the benefits and protection enjoyed by that individual. Others point out that national insurance programs are intended to have a welfare component which effectively and inevitably brings about some redistribution of income among population groups, and that is the main reason for making participation mandatory. In essence, some elements of the covered population, especially low-income groups and large families, are subsidized by other elements. If all elements of the populace are to be assured of a minimum level of income, irrespective of their personal resources, it is inevitable that eventually some groups must pay in more to the system than they will receive. Aside from that redistributional effect, inasmuch as the first generation of persons covered by a newly established social insurance program typically finance through their own, and their employers', payroll taxes only a small portion of the actuarial value of their benefits, the system generates an unfunded actuarial liability, the interest on which (assuming constant dollars, no change in the benefit structure, and no major demographic shifts) requires all succeeding generations to pay in more than they will ever receive.

This inherent conflict between social adequacy and equity was recognized from the early years of the American old-age insurance program and gave rise to substantial actuarial literature on the subject. The classic paper on the subject was written in 1938 by Reinhard A. Hohaus, an actuary of the Metropolitan Life Insurance Company and eminent student of Social Security. There is general recognition, if not a consensus, that a payroll-financed, wage-related social insurance program must be a mixture of social adequacy and individual equity—welfare versus insurance, if you will. There is no consensus as to what the relative proportions of those two components should be. Hohaus once likened the process to the formula for a dry martini. Everyone agrees that the ingredients should be gin (social adequacy) and dry vermouth (equity), but everyone has his own idea as to the exact proportions to be used. It is a matter of personal preference.

Economist Richard A. Lester of Princeton University said it well: "Unfortunately, one cannot arrive at the determination of the proper level of social insurance benefits by mathematical means, or by scientific tests, or even by pure logic. The answer depends upon one's economic and social philosophy—the sympathy he has for human misfortune, the stress he places on preserving individual dignity, and the kind of society he envisions as desirable."

Voices are being heard these days saying that the welfare and insurance components of the American social insurance system should be separated, with the welfare portion being financed out of general revenues and possibly made subject to means testing. Some call for the insurance component to be operated through the private sector. This is referred to as "privatizing" the Social Security system.

Such calls for structural "reform" of the Social Security system, coupled with past and continuing concern over the financial soundness of the system, has shaken public confidence in the linchpin of our economic security mechanism for the aged. There seems to be growing skepticism over the system's long-term capability of delivering on its promises—of honoring the so-called social contract that calls for each generation of wage earners to support the preceding generation of workers during their retirement years, in reliance upon the following generation being willing to continue the intergenerational "chain letter." Many intelligent, well-educated young people are saying, with resignation if not equanimity, that they do not expect to receive any retirement or other benefits from Social Security. If a national consensus could be reached that Social Security is to continue substantially in its present form, it is imperative that steps be promptly taken to restore confidence in the system and its long-term ability to perform its critical role.

Employer-Sponsored Programs

Sixty years before the Social Security Act was enacted the business community began to give tangible expression to its concern over the old-age financial security of the labor force by setting up more or less formal pension plans. (The early plans tended to be discretionary, reserving to the company the right to grant or discontinue pension benefits.) The motivations of the early sponsors of corporate pension plans were diverse, usually reflecting both humanitarian and business concerns. Tax minimization was not a motivating force since the federal income tax was still 40 years away. Perhaps partly for that reason, employer-sponsored pension plans spread very slowly during the preincome tax period and for many years thereafter. Another possible reason for the slow growth was the implacable opposition of the union leaders of that era, especially Samuel Gompers. The real growth of corporate pension plans began during World War II for a number of reasons, an important one being that favorable tax treatment of qualified pension plans was affirmed and expanded by the Revenue Act of 1942.

The growth in corporate pension plans—and plans for employees of state and local governments—that has occurred since then is well documented and need not be traced here. Suffice it to say that employer-sponsored pension plans now cover about 70 percent of the public and private labor force and are providing increasingly significant amounts of retirement benefits, despite the fact that, as a group, the plans are far from mature. Moreover, more than $1 trillion in assets have been accumulated to meet future pension obligations, and it has been estimated that pension plan assets will aggregate $3 trillion by 1995.

The growth in pension plans assets over the years, especially the last 20 years, has been a major source of funds for capital formation, and it should continue to serve that function. Economists generally believe that this increase in pension "wealth" of plan participants has had a dampening effect on personal savings, but the research carried out thus far, involving macroeconomic data and techniques, has not conclusively determined the extent to which pension plan saving has been a substitution for personal saving. It seems highly likely that pension plans assets have been a net addition to capital.

A number of public policy issues need to be addressed in respect of employer-sponsored pension plans. The major ones are whether pension protection should be extended to the uncovered segment of the labor force—by compulsion, if necessary; whether the percentage of covered participants that eventually become entitled to retirement benefits (vesting, portability, and reciprocity) should be expanded by legislative means; whether and how the purchasing power of accrued pension benefits, including those of terminated vested participants, should be protected; resolving the economic ownership of excess assets in a terminated defined-benefit plan; reforming the pension plan benefits insurance program (PBGC) to make it financially and actuarially sound; and easing the regulatory burden on defined-benefit plans, if they are to have a future role in providing economic security to retired persons.

In my opinion, the dominant issue is whether tax policy should continue to be used to encourage employers to establish and maintain an old-age security mechanism for their work forces. It is not clear from the legislative history that Congress ever made a clear and well-articulated decision to use tax incentives for this purpose. The present treatment of qualified plans developed over an extended period of years, through a succession of legislative and administrative actions. Some of the benefits provided under tax-favored pension plans would have had to be provided through some governmental program if the need had not been met by the private sector. To that extent so-called tax expenditures charged to tax-favored plans are gross and should be adjusted downward. It is not self-evident that tax expenditures should be used to support private-sector benefits at all income levels, particularly when a substantial segment of the labor force—and the less privileged at that—do not have access to these expenditures. Yet there may be economic side effects from private sector asset accumulation arrangements that justify tax subsidies at any income level within reason.

A separate question is, What would be the impact on existing plans and new plan formation if the present tax incentives were curtailed or eliminated? The answer to this question, of course, involves the basic motivation of employers in establishing and maintaining pension plans, whether nontax incentives are strong enough to induce employers to maintain a steady course. There are compelling nontax-related reasons why employers would want to provide retirement and other benefits to their work forces, especially if the cost can be transferred to the employees through lower wages. Dr. Ippolito's research into this phenomenon suggests that an employer's pension costs are reflected in cash wages and to a much more precise extent than has been previously demonstrated.[2] His research also documented the powerful cost-reducing effect of deferring income taxation of pension plan investment earnings. It is difficult to predict the outcome of a curtailment of existing tax preferences, and some would argue that the continued viability of the private pension institution should not be jeopardized by policy changes of unpredictable effect.

Individual Savings

There is no question that the third major source of old-age economic security, personal savings, is highly responsive to tax incentives. As is widely recognized, the savings rate in the United States is abysmally low by most reasonable standards and especially in comparison to certain other countries, notably Japan. There are undoubtedly a number of interacting reasons for the low rate of personal savings, but tax incentives would certainly be a positive force in the overall picture.

Congress recognizes the need to encourage individuals to save for their own retirement and has shown a willingness to provide tax incentives to accomplish that goal. Individual savings arrangements that enjoy favored tax treatment at the present time include IRAs, tax-deferred annuities [IRC Secs. 403(b) and 457], qualified voluntary employee contributions, and Keogh (H.R. 10) plans for self-employed persons. Employer-sponsored plans that contemplate and accommodate individual savings decisions include thrift plans and cash or deferred profit-sharing plans [Sec. 401(k) plans].

There are two major policy decisions with respect to tax-favored individual savings arrangements. One is whether they accommodate the needs and desires of all, or at least broad, segments of the population or whether they appeal primarily to the higher income elements of the population. It stands to reason that only individuals with discretionary income can take advantage of individual savings instruments, so there is bound to

[2]Richard A. Ippolito, *Pensions, Economics and Public Policy* (Homewood, Ill.: Dow Jones-Irwin, for the Pension Research Council, 1986).

be some bias toward the more fortunate members of society. For qualified plans, Congress imposes restrictions that are designed to control or minimize the utilization bias in favor of higher-income individuals. IRAs, on the other hand, are available to all employed persons and utilization is fairly broad-based. Still, as might be expected, the higher the income of the individual, the more likely he or she is to invest in an IRA.

The other policy issue is whether favorable tax treatment, particularly deductibility of contributions, should be confined to individual savings arrangements keyed to retirement needs or whether it should be accorded to any systematic savings arrangement for short-term, intermediate-term, or long-term objectives. More specifically, should the tax-favored savings instrument be structured in such a manner that the accumulated funds are available only at retirement, or should they be withdrawable at any time, subject to appropriate penalties? If the latter, should the penalties be such as to wipe out the previous tax advantages? Or should the funds be available without penalty upon retirement or in event of authentic emergencies? These are tough questions and touch on some of the most basic, and possibly immeasurable, human instincts and concerns.

From a public policy standpoint, there is a special burden on advocates of tax-favored individual savings arrangements since the potential loss of tax revenue is very great.

3

Demographic Trends Reshaping Retirement Security

by Peter K. Francese*

Millions of words have been written and spoken about the elderly in America. We read or hear about how many of them there are, how fast their numbers are growing, how poor or sick they are, and how much of the federal budget they consume. What is often missing in these monologues about the elderly is who they are and who they are not.

They are certainly not some monolithic group—an assumption implicit in much of what I hear. Some older people are rich, some are very poor, some are healthy in body and mind, others need vast amounts of medical care. Many live alone, others with a spouse or family, but quite a few are institutionalized in nursing homes or hospitals. Then there are people we would classify as elderly according to their age who have full-time jobs and do not consider themselves old at all.

Clearly, any discussion of economic security in retirement must first recognize that we are talking about a diverse multidimensional population that has a whole array of wants and needs and is changing even as we speak about it. The demo-

*President, American Demographics, Inc.

graphic dimensions of the elderly that impact on their economic security are three: their age distribution, their income characteristics, and their family structure.

Age Distribution

Because of the decennial census program and CPS of the Bureau of the Census (as well as their population projection series), we know a great deal about the age structure of older persons. There are three main groups: 65 to 74, 75 to 84, 85 plus. From the same source, we know something about their income and a little about their assets from which income can be derived.

Family structure can also be obtained from census data, but the dynamic nature of American families is more fully revealed in longitudinal studies such as those conducted by the Institute for Social Research at the University of Michigan. There are three major household types: married couples, other families, and nonfamilies—essentially people who live alone. Before discussing the dimensions of these types, let's consider their absolute and relative size.

The United States is the fourth largest country in the world, in terms of both land area and population. But it is also one of the slowest growing. For the last 30 years, it has been growing at a progressively slower rate, which is currently just about 1 percent per year. In about the middle of the next century, the Census Bureau projects that we will reach zero population growth. Already two of our regions—the Northeast and the Midwest—have had zero growth periods in the last decade.

One inevitable consequence of very slow population increase is an aging population. In 1980, our median age was exactly 30; by 2000 it will be over 36. This rising median age is pushed along by an accelerating life expectancy. People who turn 65 today can expect to live into their early 80s, between a year and two years longer than they would have lived only a decade ago. The result has been an elderly segment whose numbers are growing more than twice as fast as the rest of the population. To quote Sam Preston, "Between 1971 and 1981, the elderly population of the U.S. grew faster than the population of India." What has been the effect of these differential growth rates on the population distribution?

In 1955, when the baby boom was about at its loudest, the elderly were only about 9 percent of the total population, while children were exactly one third. That still left 58 percent in the traditional wage-earning years, 18 to 64. Today, children have shrunk to one quarter, while the elderly have grown to only 12 percent. The net result has been to increase the wage earners to 62 percent. This relative distribution (children at one quarter, elderly at one eighth) is not expected to change significantly for the next two and a half decades.

In 2000, according to the middle series projection by the Census Bureau, the elderly will be 13 percent and children will still be at 25 percent. The ratio between workers and dependents appears fairly stable until the baby boom starts to retire in about 30 years.

Many writers have raised the specter of financial catastrophe when the baby boom retires, but several things can happen between now and 30 years in the future that could radically alter the population distribution or economic situation for the elderly.

For example, immigration from Latin America may be higher than expected. In 1950 there were approximately the same number of people in North America (United States and Canada) as in Latin America (everything from the Mexican border south). By the year 2000 there will be two and one half times as many people there as here, and Mexico City is expected to be the largest urban area in the world. The median age in Mexico is 18. With our rising median age and decreasing proportion of young people, it is foolishness not to expect much more immigration from Latin America than the 400,000 a year built into the official long-range population projections. Immigration might be a major factor for our economic security in a generation.

Of far more immediate interest in terms of economic security is the changing demography of the elderly, in particular their age distribution. A generation ago, two thirds of the elderly were 65 to 74 years old, about a quarter (27 percent) were 75 to

84, and only 5 percent were 85 or older—a group known as the very old. By 1970, the shift toward the top end of the age scale became evident with those over 75 increasing their share and those under 75 decreasing. Today, approximately 1 in 10 elderly persons is over 85 years, nearly a third are 75 to 84, and the youngest cohort has shrunk to under 60 percent.

By the year 2000, we see the effects of a generation and a half of better medical care and better living standards for the elderly, combined with the smaller cohort of those born during the Depression reaching retirement age. One in seven elderly are 85 or older, more than a third are 75 to 84, and only about half are 65 to 74. The youngest age group, which is the healthiest and is the least in need of economic assistance, has shrunk from two thirds to half the elderly population, while those in greatest need of personal and medical care are becoming a larger and larger fraction of the elderly.

The most rapidly growing age group in America is people 85 years old and over. From a tiny group of less than a million in 1955, the very old now exceed 2.5 million in number and are expected to total 5 million in only 15 years. Today, quoting Barbara Torrey, "The federal government provides an estimated $50 billion in benefits and services to the . . . very old. . . . These are more benefits than are given for all the nonaged poor; it is also twice what is spent today for total veterans' benefits or unemployment benefits in the United States."

We don't have to wait for the baby boom to retire for economic catastrophe. For example, today only about 20 percent of those over 85 are in nursing homes. But 20 percent of the increase of 2.2 million very old people means nearly half a million new nursing home beds. The average nursing home has about 100 beds. So that means we must construct 5,000 new nursing homes or approximately one every day for the next 15 years. Clearly, an alternative to institutionalizing one fifth of the very old must be found. The obvious answer is home care, but as we will see when we look at family structure, the obvious does not always work.

When we talk about elderly, we are talking about a group that is predominantly, and as we go up in age progressively, women. Because women outlive men by about eight years and because women tend to marry older men, there are only 67 elderly men for every 100 elderly women. Even so, only 57 percent of the people 65 to 74 are women. But at ages 75 to 84, nearly two thirds (63 percent) of the people are women; and among the very old, aged 85 and over, 74 percent—almost three fourths—of the population are women. Among the very old, there are only 38 men for every 100 women.

This unbalanced sex distribution has important economic consequences. People who are 85 and older now or will turn 85 years old between now and 2000 were in their working years when the world of work was almost exclusively the world of men. They had few opportunities to earn a significant wage base for Social Security or become eligible for employer-sponsored pensions or learn much about financial matters. This will not be the case when baby-boom women retire. Most of them will have spent their adult years at work. Most of them will either have private pensions or IRAs or both and will hardly be ignorant of financial matters.

Income Characteristics

So it is not just the number of elderly in each age group that's important, it's also their second demographic dimension, financial condition. The latest income figures we have are from the 1985 Current Population Survey taken last March by the Census Bureau. It shows the median household income of the elderly last year was the lowest of any age group. It was $12,800, or just 57 percent of the median for all households ($22,400). The household income of the elderly is even lower than that of the youngest households (under age 25) which traditionally have low incomes because they are just entering the work force. Looking at just these figures, one might conclude that the elderly are among the poorest Americans and therefore in need of greater federal assistance. But the picture is more complex than just median household income, because elderly households are so much smaller than those of other age groups.

There is an average of 271 people in every 100 households, but where the householder is 65 years old or older, there are only 176 people in every 100 households. By dividing the average household income for each age group by the number of persons in each of the households, the per-person income for the elderly rises from 57 percent to 103 percent of the average for all households. It turns out that elderly households have an average of $10,400 per person, or more than all the households younger than 45. The poorest households turn out to be the youngest ones (under 25 years old), which earn only $7,300 per person, and the wealthiest are those preretirement households 55 to 64. Furthermore, we can presume that because of lower housing costs, the elderly's $10,400 buys a lot more than the $7,300 of the youngest households.

Because the Current Population Survey is too small a sample to obtain income for the very old, it is necessary to go back to the 1980 census. Barbara Torrey of the Census Bureau has tabulated income by age and found what we would expect to find—that the youngest elderly had more income than the oldest. Those persons over age 85 had only 64 percent of the income of people 65 to 69. That's not surprising considering the fact that about 25 percent of the men and 15 percent of the women in that younger age group are still in the labor force. The fact remains, however, that those who need the most in the way of medical care have the least ability to pay for it themselves. Ms. Torrey also found that net worth in terms of home equity, financial, and other assets declines with advancing age.

One contributing factor to a higher income is education. Generally speaking, the higher one's educational attainment, the higher one's lifetime earnings will be. In 1970 only about 1 in 10 adults had a college degree and only about one third of elderly persons had even graduated from high school. Today nearly 20 percent of adults are college graduates. But only 10 percent of those over 65 are college graduates.

The growing elderhostel program—now available at over 700 colleges and universities—is contributing to closing the education gap. William Lazer, writing in *American Demographics,* feels that within 10 years over one quarter of the elderly will have had some college education.

The future economic security of the elderly depends not just on their income, however we measure it, but on how they manage the income and assets they have. Increasing educational attainment will make the difference between fear of poverty and understanding financial management. And it may make the difference between a barely adequate income and true economic security.

One important measure of economic progress is the reverse of economic security—poverty. The poverty rate—the percentage of people living in poverty—is measured by the Census Bureau every year. According to the federal definition of this condition, the percentage of all persons in poverty remained quite constant, in the 11 to 12 percent range, all during the 1970s. Since 1980, however, it has risen dramatically so that last year 14 percent (one in seven Americans) lived in poverty. In the last five years, we have added the equivalent of the state of New Jersey (7 million people) to the poverty rolls.

None of that increase can be attributed to the elderly poor—quite the contrary. In 1969 a quarter of those over 65 years old lived in poverty, but by 1979 only 15 percent did. 1982 was a historic year: For the first time in history the elderly poverty rate fell below the rate for all persons. It continues to fall and is presently two percentage points lower than the average for all persons. Only one in eight persons over age 65 lives in poverty.

Then where is this increase in poverty coming from? From children. Fifteen years ago, the poverty rate for children was only 13.8 percent, close to that of all persons. It has risen steadily since then and now stands at 21 percent. More than one in five children lives in poverty.

Family Structure

Most children, like most adults, live in families—58 percent of American households are husband-wife families—but those with no children now outnumber those with children, and that almost mythical family (mom, pop, and two kids) is only 11 percent. About 15 percent of households are other families—mostly single parents—while nearly one quarter of all households are people who live alone.

If we look at young elderly households, we see that almost the same percentage of households are married couples (52 percent as opposed to 58 percent) and about 9 percent are other families. But nearly one third of households 65 to 74 are women who live alone. Compare this to households 75 years old and older. The majority (56 percent) are people who live alone. Forty-five percent—nearly half—of all households age 75 or older are women who live alone. Only one third of the households of those 75 and over are married couples and only 11 percent are other families.

It is very difficult to deliver home care to a person who lives alone. It's a paradox that the older people get, the more dependent they are on others, the less money they have, the fewer their assets, and yet more of them live alone. It is another paradox that at a time of increasing longevity and the abandonment of mandatory retirement ages, more people are retiring early. For example, among men aged 55 to 64, over 80 percent were in the labor force 15 years ago; now it is less than 70 percent and is expected to be only two thirds by 1990. Just when we might expect people to continue working in anticipation of many years in retirement, they appear to be doing exactly the opposite.

Some of these people who are retiring now and who will retire in the next 15 to 20 years are parents of Baby Boomers. They gave birth to the Baby Boomers at a time when divorce was an unusual occurrence, single parents were rare, only a few children lived in poverty, and the dominant form of household was a husband, a nonworking wife, and two or more children.

Yet their children, those people who might be expected to assist their parents in old age, live vastly different lives. Divorce is commonplace and so are single parents. For the last five years, the most rapidly growing household types have been single parents and people who live alone. During those years the only age group that actually increased its income in inflation-adjusted dollars was the elderly.

Various proposals have been made for intergenerational cost-sharing for the support of the elderly. These proposals generally rest on the foundation that there are lots of Baby Boomers, each of whom can contribute something to the support of aged parents and in some cases grandparents. Considering the poor economic circumstances that many young people live in and the decline in real earnings growth that Baby Boomers are experiencing, I doubt that their contribution can be as large as their numbers would suggest.

Summary

Well, where do these trends lead us? What do they tell us about the future of economic security for retired persons? I leave you with three thoughts and one comment.

First, the elderly are generally not poor, and in fact appear to be improving their own economic condition year by year. But the very old are the least well off, have the fewest assets, and yet have the greatest need for health and personal care.

Second, most elderly people today are women who grew up at a time when women were not expected to continue in school, or have careers outside their home, or concern themselves with the management of financial resources. We should not be surprised if they are overly fearful of poverty, are vulnerable to fraud, and seem incapable of providing for their own economic security, even with what may appear to be adequate assets. It is unlikely that the generation that succeeds them will be in the same position.

Third, the dramatic growth in number of the very old means an increase in elderly people who are in their last year of life. It is this last year of life that has consumed a disproportionate share of medical expenses in a futile attempt to prolong life. One answer has been the growing hospicare movement and the concept of living wills. It is possible that in our purely demographic efforts to extrapolate past trends concerning the very elderly and the potentially enormous cost of that growth that we forget society's ability to respond with an innovation or a new idea and change the outcome.

Finally, we should keep in mind that the economic security of the elderly is much more than a demographic matter. It is a social and cultural matter, an allocation of economic resources matter, and above all a political matter. One out of every three voters is 55 years old or over. Less than half of people under 35 bother to go to the polls, but more than 70 percent of those 55 and older vote, no doubt early and often. With that kind of voting record among the elderly, I don't think the matter of their economic security will be entirely left up to younger people like me.

4

Pensions and Economics: Towards an Efficient Retirement Policy

by Richard A. Ippolito*

The purpose of this chapter is to evaluate government policy towards retirement income, especially pensions. The federal government has been setting policy for the nation's retirement system for over 60 years.[1] This policy has taken the form of Social Security, tax rules, and elaborate regulations. The results have been dramatic. Tax policy alone is largely responsible for the trillion dollars in assets held by private pension plans in 1984 (see Appendix). Two thirds of the current work force will collect pensions replacing 25 percent of the final wage (besides Social Security). The question, however, is not whether government retirement policy is effective, but rather whether it is effective in attaining the goals set out by the citizenry for the long run.

Any evaluation of policy requires a benchmark, an ideal against which current policy can be evaluated. In this chapter

---

*Director of Research, Pension Program, U.S. Department of Labor. The views expressed in this chapter are those of the author and do not represent the position of the U.S. Department of Labor.

[1]Arguably their involvement started with the Revenue Act of 1921, which established the basic tax policy towards pensions that prevails today. Also, see note 5.

it is assumed that the goal of government policy is not to enforce particular replacement rates during retirement, nor to set retirement ages, nor to write pension contracts, nor to control savings rates; but rather that its purpose is to engender the efficient allocation of resources.

More specifically, a sound national policy for retirement income is not one that prescribes retirement conditions. It is one that offers least interference with the natural allocation of resources for retirement among firms and workers, subject only to provisions that the government may 1) address nonsavers' tendencies to free-ride on savers, and 2) enforce private market contracts. This chapter evalutes some of the principal government policies that affect retirement income in the United States. The goal is to determine which policies are consistent with this national policy and to recommend changes in public laws that fall outside its bounds.

In pursuing this exercise, the temptation to recommend "optimum" policies is avoided if these changes are considered infeasible. For example, an argument can be made that the Social Security system was a mistake, that a mandatory minimum national pension system would have ensured that all citizens saved a minimum amount to support retirement consumption without causing the nation to forgo the huge capital accumulation engendered by the pay-as-you-go Social Security system.[2] But for this chapter it is assumed that the Social Security system is here to stay in essentially its current form and level. Feasible alterations in the program that contribute to greater overall efficiency of the retirement system, however, are discussed in some detail.

Likewise, it is taken as given that the United States will maintain a comprehensive income tax system. Proposals to alter the system to an expenditure tax system (a national sales tax), while defensible and supported by many public finance economists, is avoided here.[3] Some of the principles of this tax

---

[2]These issues are addressed in Martin Feldstein, "Social Security, Induced Retirement and Aggregate Capital Accumulation," *Journal of Political Economy* 82 (September 1974), 905–26.

[3]See, for example, David E. Bradford, "The Case for a Personal Consumption Tax," in *What Should Be Taxed: Income or Expenditure?* ed., Joseph Pechman (Washington, D.C.: Brookings Institution, 1980), pp. 75–113.

system are already in place in the form of pension tax policy; and it will be shown that modifications in pension regulations can generate most of the efficiency gains of an expenditure tax, at least with regard to savings for retirement. If an expenditure tax replaced the income tax system, pensions in anything like their current size would not survive.[4]

This chapter concentrates on the most important elements of public pension policy: pension tax policy, pension regulation, and pension insurance. Should this body of policy be modified and, if so, in which ways? Each point is discussed in turn, culminating in a list of prescriptions for a more efficient retirement policy in the United States.

Pension Tax Policy

Special treatment of pensions in the tax structure in the United States is a major ingredient of federal pension and retirement policy. By enacting the Revenue Act of 1921,[5] the government set the stage for the spread of pensions after World War II, when a radical change in the structure of income tax rates and coverage took place. A central feature of pension tax law from an efficiency standpoint is that earnings in the pension trust fund are tax exempt during the accumulation period.[6] This special tax rule toward pension savings has a major impact on individuals' decisions to save for retirement.

Distortions Imposed by the Double Tax on Nonpension Savings

An example will clarify the tax implications of the tax-exempt pension status. For simplicity, suppose the tax structure is proportional, not progressive. Consider the simple case of a defined-contribution plan. In lieu of some portion of cash

[4]In such a system, all savings vehicles would be taxed equally, and hence no preference would be available for pensions.

[5]The Revenue Act of 1921 permitted deduction of pension contributions at the corporate level, tax-free accumulations within pension funds, and deferral of personal income taxation on pensions until retirement.

[6]The law also permits deferment of pension contributions as taxable income to the worker until he actually receives the contributions in the form of pension benefits. This confers sizable income-smoothing benefits in a progressive income tax scheme.

wages, the firm contributes a portion of the worker's earnings into a defined-contribution account; upon retirement a lump sum amount is available to the worker. Compare this method of saving for retirement to one where the individual saves for retirement outside the pension plan. The firm can deduct either wages or pension contributions at the corporate level; so the firm's tax liability is independent of the form in which its workers receive total compensation. Not so for workers.

Consider a typical worker who faces a proportional personal tax rate of 33 percent. Suppose the worker can choose whether his firm can add $100 to the cash wage per year or contribute $100 to a defined-contribution plan. If the worker does *not* use the pension plan, the $100 "extra" wage is assessed a 33 percent personal income tax, leaving $67 free to save. Suppose the inflation rate and the interest rate are each 10 percent (the real interest rate is zero).[7] Consider a particular year in the worker's tenure, for example, 15 years prior to retirement.

The $67 will not grow at the rate of 10 percent. Savings outside the pension program are subject to the personal income tax; thus, the after-tax interest rate is 6.67 percent. After 15 years, the $67 savings is worth $182 in after-tax income. But since the inflation rate is 10 percent, the real value of $182 in year-15 dollars expressed in year-1 dollars is $41. If the worker chooses to accept the $100 cash wage, he has $67 after tax to spend immediately. If the worker saves the $67 through a tax-exposed vehicle instead, he ends up with the equivalent of $41 to spend during retirement. The double tax on savings favors more current spending and less saving.

Suppose the pension plan is used instead. If $100 is deposited into the pension plan, no immediate tax is assessed; instead it is assessed as taxable income at retirement. During the accumulation period, interest earned in the pension plan is tax exempt. Thus, the $100 grows at the gross-of-tax rate of 10 percent per year, not the after-tax rate of 6.67 percent. After 15 years, the $100 is worth $448, which is subject to the propor-

---

[7]If the inflation rate is zero but the real interest rate is 10 percent, similar results obtain but they are somewhat less intuitive.

Table 4–1
Savings Distortion of the Double Tax: Illustration

$100 Compensation Taken in Form of	*Spend Income in Year*	*After-Tax Interest Rate*	*After-Tax Value of $100 in*	
			Year 15	*Year 1*
Cash (spend now)	1	—	—	$67
Cash (nonpension savings)	15	6.7%	$182	41
Pension	15	10.0	300	67

Example assumes that worker faces a constant 33 percent marginal tax rate; the inflation rate and the nominal interest rate are 10 percent (the real interest rate is zero).

tional 33 percent tax. After the tax is assessed, $300 (= $448 × .67) in after-tax income is available to the worker.[8] In year-1 dollars, $300 in year-15 dollars is worth $67. If the worker chooses to accept the $100 cash wage, he has $67 after tax to spend immediately. If the worker saves the $100 in a pension plan, he ends up with the equivalent of $67 to spend during retirement. The pension eliminates the double tax on savings. The pension and nonpension scenarios are depicted in Table 4–1.

By eliminating the double tax on savings, pensions remove the distortion in the tax code favoring spending now and saving less for retirement. By "neutralizing" the decision to save for retirement—that is, by eliminating the double-tax distortion—pension tax policy offsets biases in the income tax system that induce workers to take shorter retirements and to have lower standards of living during retirement.[9]

---

[8]This is equivalent to the worker being assessed a 33 percent tax on his $100 savings immediately but then having the opportunity to earn the full 10 percent interest rate on his savings. That is, at a 10 percent interest rate, $67 grows to $300 in year 15. Viewing the pension tax advantage in this way, it is clear that the value of the pension is not that the income tax is escaped or deferred, but rather that it exempts this savings from the so-called second tax during the accumulation period.

[9]Moreover, it can be shown that once tax progressivity is introduced, pension tax policy offsets additional potentially serious distortions on hours worked and age of retirement. See Richard A. Ippolito, "Income Tax Policy and Lifetime Labor Supply," *Journal of Public Economics* 26 (April 1985), pp. 327–47.

Evaluation of Pension Tax Policy

The removal of the double-tax distortion improves economic efficiency because workers are not *artificially* discouraged from their optimal choice of retirement age and retirement consumption. They are free to make retirement choices without influence from the federal government. But just because pension tax policy has led to an undistorted retirement pattern, this does not mean that pension tax preference is unambiguously more efficient, in the sense of reducing the costs of overall distortions imposed by tax policy.

The ambiguity is primarily attributable to other distortions that may be created by attempts to replace lost revenue on interest income by raising taxes elsewhere. For example, if adoption of an expenditure tax means higher personal tax rates to generate equal revenue, workers may work less because work will be more heavily taxed.

In the case of pensions, however, it is unclear that any ambiguity exists. It is arguable that the tax revenue lost by reducing taxation on pension savings is at least partially offset by consequent reductions in public expenditures on old-age retirement and welfare systems. In other words, raising taxes on pensions may so discourage private capital accumulation for retirement that the government will face substantially higher burdens to *publicly* support more retirement consumption. If this is the case, the ambiguity remaining around the pension tax treatment is substantially reduced.

Personal Income Tax Treatment of Social Security Contributions

If current tax treatment of private pensions is good public policy from the perspective of economic efficiency, it is reasonable to wonder why the same tax policy is not applied to the main competing system for producing retirement income: Social Security. The U.S. tax code influences the individual's implicit choice for pensions compared to Social Security. The Social Security system is technically a mandatory program for most workers, but presumably its size is determined by aggregate implicit demand. While this demand is affected by numerous factors, the current size of the system could be too large owing to the peculiar way in which Social Security contributions and benefits are treated in the U.S. tax system.

Presumably, public and private pensions are alternative vehicles to attain the same goal: to provide a means to save for retirement consumption. But the tax code does not treat Social Security and private pension contributions and benefits in the same way. It was shown above that the tax treatment afforded private pensions can be rationalized on the basis of efficiency because it imposes neutrality between immediate and postponed consumption. Peculiarly, the same tax treatment has not been extended to the Social Security system.

If tax policy toward Social Security were applied to private pensions, it would be easy to demonstrate that workers would be induced artificially to save too much compared to an undistorted choice.[10] In addition, because the tax code treats private pensions and Social Security differently, it induces individuals to prefer a combination of public *and* private pension schemes even though one alone might be preferred otherwise.[11]

This subtle aspect of the U.S. tax code may play a significant role in the comparative sizes of the Social Security and private pension systems. Even if individuals clearly preferred either private pensions or Social Security, they would still rationally choose a combination of the schemes to minimize their lifetime tax burden. This distortion easily can be eliminated by ensuring that the tax treatment of Social Security contributions are identical to the tax treatment afforded private pension contributions.

All Social Security contributions (including employee contributions) should be deductible for tax purposes at the time they are contributed, and all Social Security benefits should be taxed at the time they are received. In this way, tax policy toward all retirement income conforms to the properties of an expenditure tax (the decision to spend or save is not distorted). Further, the distortion of the choice between private pensions and Social Security caused by the imposition of different tax treatments on

---

[10]This occurs because 50 percent of all contributions to retirement consumption are tax-exempt. All current consumption would be subject to the full income tax.

[11]This distortion is demonstrated in Richard A. Ippolito, *Pensions, Economics and Public Policy* (Homewood, Ill.: Dow Jones-Irwin, A Pension Research Council monograph, 1986), chap. 12.

retirement income depending on the savings vehicle chosen is eliminated.

In 1984, an equivalent of this solution was introduced into the tax code but only if the income of a (married) worker exceeded $32,000. That is, while half the contributions to Social Security are still deductible, one half the benefits are now subject to tax (for high-income families). This solution should be modified to incorporate the solution to *all* retirees. The personal and standard deductions and the progressive nature of the tax schedule already insulate low-income retirees from the assessment of any substantial tax on their Social Security benefits.

Private Pensions versus Individual Retirement Accounts

While a strong case can be made in favor of special tax treatment of pension savings for retirement, it is unfortunate that this tax treatment was (and to some extent still is) tied to firm-operated private pensions. Prior to 1974, savings for retirement were eligible for tax-preferable treatment only if they were made through a private (or public) pension plan. ERISA made Individual Retirement Accounts (IRAs) available to individuals who were not covered by private pensions and, beginning in 1982, IRAs were made available to individuals already covered by a private pension. All IRAs, however, are subject to (nominal) contribution limits that may be constraining either currently or in the future as inflation takes its toll on the limits now set.

By historically tying the availability of the special tax treatment to firm pensions, imperfections that have distorted individual choice have been introduced into the tax system. Partly for administrative cost reasons and partly because of Internal Revenue Service rules (which are discussed below), firm pension rules are applied across broad segments of the firm's labor force. Ruling out perfect matching between individuals and firms, individuals under the current code will typically settle for implicit savings rates that differ from their preferred savings rates.

The imperfections in the current tax code that discriminate in favor of firm-sponsored pensions are easily remedied. Contribution restrictions on IRAs should be eliminated, putting them on par from a tax perspective with private pension systems.[12] Private pensions would then be required to compete with a system that would offer individuals substantial flexibility in rearranging their income flow over life.[13]

The introduction of salary-reduction 401(k) plans and the introduction of limited IRAs to pension-covered workers in the Economic Recovery Tax Act of 1981 represent steps toward attaining this solution. Firms can now offer workers the opportunity to contribute variable amounts to a 401(k) plan without requiring (though permitting) matching firm contributions. Combined employer and employee contributions up to 25 percent of salary are tax deductible (subject to a $30,000 limit). Though the plans are again tied to the firm and are still subject to IRS discrimination laws, 401(k)s represent a significant step toward establishing a more efficient voluntary private pension system; so do the expanded IRAs.

The popularity of these new provisions is a testament to workers' preference for more freedom in their savings choices for retirement. If pension plans were not constraining, the new plans would not have been popular. But estimated IRA assets have increased from zero in 1974 to $132 billion in 1984, including $32 billion in contributions in 1983 alone. Assets in 401(k) plans have increased from $6 billion in 1974 to $42 in 1984.[14]

An unconstrained IRA system, combined with the deregulation of pensions (see below), sets the stage for removing firms from the business of managing savings accounts, entrusting this function instead to institutions specializing in money management. Firms will remain in the pension business only insofar as pensions affect productivity for at least some workers. Oth-

---

[12]Actually, IRS rules limit contributions to private defined-benefit pension plans to be consistent with annuities that are roughly $90,000 per year. Alternatively, IRS rules permit contributions up to $30,000 per year in defined-contribution plans. IRAs could be subject to similar limits.

[13]IRAs can be set up in ways that replicate the annuity features of defined-benefit pensions. See Ippolito, *Pensions, Economics and Public Policy*, chap. 12.

[14]See Lynn Rockwell, "Trends in Nontraditional Pension Savings," U.S. Department of Labor, mimeo, 1985.

erwise, the retirement savings function will be disentangled from the worker-firm relationship.[15]

Constraints on Nonfiduciary Pension Rules

Public policies affecting pension equilibrium are not limited to those surrounding the U.S. tax code. The federal government has had a long-standing influence on the structure of pension plans through Internal Revenue Service discrimination rules and, more recently, ERISA. Moreover, public policy has indirectly influenced the way in which pensions can be structured to influence retirement ages or incentives for workers to quit the firm prior to retirement age. Public policies that influence the way in which firms structure their pension plans are considered in this section.

IRS Discrimination Rules

Internal Revenue Service rules make it difficult for firms to tailor pensions to fit the heterogeneity of the work force. Since the Revenue Act of 1942, the IRS has imposed discrimination rules on firm pensions. In essence, firms cannot offer different pension plans to different types of employees, especially if the groups differ systematically by wage level. Firms must offer roughly comparable pensions to virtually all employees in the firm.

Discrimination rules have virtually ensured that inefficient wage contracts will be negotiated. To the extent that the firm is merely facilitating tax deferrals or annuity savings for its workers, it is required by law to impose savings rates that are virtually identical across the firm. To the extent that the firm finds it

[15]It can be legitimately argued that incorporating a policy of unconstrained IRAs into the tax code could lead to an arbitrage system of sorts, resulting in a systematic raid on the U.S. Treasury. The potential for arbitrage arises because IRA accounts can accumulate interest on a tax-sheltered basis, yet individuals can deduct interest on their personal income tax returns on money borrowed in the market. It can be shown that the potential for arbitrage is sharply reduced by progressivity in the U.S. tax structure. See Ippolito, *Pensions, Economics and Public Policy*, chap. 12. But to eliminate it entirely, it would be necessary to eliminate the deduction for interest on borrowed money, a policy that could be justified independent of its relation to the IRA scheme. That is, tax deductability of interest payments results in incentives to individuals to borrow "too much."

optimal to penalize early-outs for some types of employees (e.g., supervisors or other highly compensated employees) but not necessarily others (perhaps low-paid workers), it is forced to apply some compromised strategy to all workers.

A policy should be adopted to keep private pensions comparable with IRAs and to allow firms to tailor penalties to particular groups of employees: all IRS discrimination laws should be repealed. Firms should be permitted to (1) offer employees the option to contribute to the pension plan at variable rates; these voluntary contributions should be given the same tax treatment as IRAs and private pension contributions; and (2) offer stylized pension plans to different groups of workers without regard to wage levels.

The introduction of 401(k) plans represents a positive step in the direction of offering more flexibility in the private pension system. They enable the firm to offer significantly more flexibility on the upside to workers who wish to save more than the primary pension plan permits. By adjusting the primary plan downward over time, the combination of the primary plan and the 401(k) can generate the efficient kinds of results discussed here. But the overall result of these plans is still subject to IRS discrimination rules which in effect rule out this option if the result is skewed in favor of high-wage earners saving "too much" relative to low-wage earners.

ERISA Pension Rules

In many ways, ERISA can be viewed in a dichotomous way. On the one hand, the law acts to insure pension promises against mismanagement, fraud, and bankruptcy.[16] The law provides explicit insurance through the Pension Benefit Guaranty Corporation; the Corporation partially insures promised benefits to participants of terminated defined-benefit plans.[17] The

[16]The law also has included certain reporting and disclosure provisions which are not included in the discussion.

[17]As currently structured, the portion of real benefits guaranteed is a function of the inflation rate. Since the insurance guarantees nominal liabilities at the time of plan termination, these benefits erode in real terms by the time the pension benefits are paid out. The insurance therefore is far from complete.

insurance is accompanied by a monitoring of fiduciary aspects of plans presumably to reduce the moral hazard potential created by the insurance.

On the other hand, ERISA acts to constrain the fundamental rules of a pension. In particular the law requires (1) that all employees age 21 and over with at least one year of service, be covered by the pension plan; (2) that all employees vest within 15 years; and (3) that all vested benefits are nonforfeitable. The first rule goes toward encouraging the firm to treat all employees alike, even if young employees do not find it optimal to contribute to pension plans. The last two rules go toward constraining the penalties that firms can impose on individuals who leave the firm early.

Vesting rules preclude complete forfeiture of employees' benefits when they leave the firm prematurely except when departure occurs prior to 15 years of service. Nonforfeiture rules ensure that workers receive at least the nominal benefits they have accrued prior to their departure. They therefore lose a portion of their "real" benefits, but additional penalties are precluded. ERISA rules presumably work to ensure that private pensions operate more like savings accounts, rather than as devices to affect worker performance.

In the absence of IRAs, the government conditions tax-deferral benefits on participation in private pensions. A case might be made that it behooves the government to protect individuals who might be induced by this policy to accept risks they otherwise would not accept if the same tax advantage were available outside the firm. If IRAs are available to everyone, however, these arguments are difficult to justify. Under this scenario, since individuals can obtain the same tax advantages afforded pensions by investing in IRAs, it can be reasonably presumed that they will participate in a private pension only if the efficiency effects generated by pensions outweigh the associated pension penalties.

Given the availability of unconstrained IRAs, there should be no constraints on the firm's choice of participation, vesting, or penalty provisions. Firms should have the freedom to arrange their pension plans in any way they wish, subject only to adequate disclosure to employees on a regular basis. Such disclosure is now required by ERISA.

Policy Influences on the Retirement Age

Federal policy constrains firms' abilities to design the pension in such a way that an appropriate schedule of costs is set for workers who do not leave the firm "on time." In particular, firms cannot stylize pensions and pension rules for certain employees. Moreover, congressional and other proposals have sought to directly constrain firms' abilities to affect overall retirement ages; for example, consider proposals that would require firms to continue counting service in the pension formula past the normal retirement age or require actuarially fair adjustments no matter how "late" the worker chooses to retire.[18] Given old-age discrimination laws and restrictions against mandatory retirement ages prior to age 70, firms have little flexibility to influence the retirement of workers who, on average, lose their productive capability as they age.

The federal government itself has imposed penalties on workers who want to work past age 65 (and firms that want to keep workers). It has done this by imposing an implicit tax on Social Security benefits for individuals who work past age 65 or retire prior to age 62.[19]

In the past, if the individual chose to retire either before age 62 or especially after age 65, he faced a significant actuarial penalty; in essence, workers may have been induced to retire either "too soon" or "too late" compared to their preferred retirement date.[20] In addition, production inefficiencies may also accompany the tax.

The implicit Social Security tax on work at older ages may inhibit firms from inducing retirement outside the 62–65 Social Security retirement age "window." Maximum labor productivity in some firms may depend on substantial investment ("training") periods during the worklife and an accompanying

[18]Most pensions are not actuarially fair after "normal" retirement age (usually age 65); hence, workers are offered strong incentives not to stay with the firm beyond this age. For example, the Equal Employment Opportunity Commission recently proposed a regulation (46 Federal Register 43848) to require all pension plans to continue service accruals beyond the normal retirement age.

[19]See, for example, Richard Burkhauser, "The Early Acceptance of Social Security: An Asset Maximizing Approach," *Industrial Labor Relations Review* 33 (July 1980), pp. 484–92.

[20]Ibid.

lengthy worklife to reap the full benefits of the investments. Effective Social Security taxation at older ages distorts these types of labor contracts. If firms find it efficient to keep workers at older ages, they must in effect reimburse them for incurring the effective tax imposed by the Social Security system. It is expensive to write private pension rules that are inconsistent with the age 65 (or earlier) bias imposed by the Social Security system. Repeal of this implicit tax would eliminate the penalties imposed on writing more diverse private pension rules and wage contracts, and therefore would lead to potentially large gains in efficiency.

In fact, Congress has scheduled the effective elimination of this implicit Social Security tax beginning in 2010. It has also indexed wages in the formula to a labor market wage index, thereby removing the tax on workers wishing to retire prior to age 62.[21] These represent positive steps toward removing artificial obstacles in the path of voluntary decisions to retire. These decisions should be made by workers and firms in the private sector, without influence from the Social Security system. The effective removal of the earnings test makes it more likely that retirement will occur when workers and firms decide it is most efficient to do so.

The federal government should remove itself from the business of influencing retirement patterns in the labor force. The elimination of the implicit Social Security tax should be effected immediately, not in 25 years. And the government should not attempt to regulate private pension rules affecting the retirement age.

Federal Pension Insurance

Depending on the theory of ERISA insurance, it is either easy or difficult to recommend the abolishment of the Pension Benefit Guaranty Corporation. If, on the one hand, ERISA was created for the benefit of comparatively poorly funded, unprofitable firms at the expense of well-funded, profitable firms, it is easy from an efficiency viewpoint to recommend its elimination.

[21]See "Social Security Amendments of 1983: Legislative History and Summary of Provisions," *Social Security Bulletin*, July 1983.

Some research has supported this view of ERISA.[22] If, on the other hand, pensions are considered the equivalent of guaranteed future wage contracts, it is easy to recommend the replacement of ERISA insurance with a change in bankruptcy laws that makes pension promises the equivalent of wages. There may, however, be legitimate reasons for ERISA insurance to exist and, if so, elimination of the insurance may lead to a reduction in efficiency.[23]

One change, however, can be made regardless of the theory of ERISA that ultimately prevails: The insurance premiums assessed by the Pension Benefit Guaranty Corporation should be set in relation to the risk exposure each plan gives to the corporation, and they should be free of any subsidies from taxpayers as a whole over the long term. One easy way to accomplish this is to mandate pension plans to find insurance against legal liabilities in the private insurance market, letting these firms set competitive premium levels according to risk exposure.

Fiduciary rules, including funding and investment guidelines, would be determined competitively, not arbitrarily and perhaps inefficiently, by the federal government. The federal government could reinsure these liabilities at an appropriate premium to ensure that insurance firms would remain solvent even through catastrophic temporal episodes. Because of selectivity problems, the mandatory nature of the insurance could be maintained. If the corporation is maintained, it should mimic rates that would exist in the private market if ERISA insurance were "privatized."

Currently, pension plans that are 150 percent funded (in a termination sense) and are sponsored by firms in high-growth industries pay the same premium as those that are 50 percent funded and are in contracting industries. None seemingly pay true economic insurance premiums.[24] The existence of the

---

[22]See Ippolito, *Pensions, Economics and Public Policy*, chaps. 10 and 11.

[23]Some legitimate theories of ERISA are discussed elsewhere. See Ippolito, *Pensions, Economics and Public Policy*, Appendix 12–2.

[24]At the time of this writing, firms paid insurance premiums equal to $2.60 per participant per year. A proposal was pending that would raise this premium to $8.50. But it is unlikely that even this premium is economic because, among other things, it is based on the assumptions that no large plans will ever terminate and that nominal interest rate will remain in double digits.

cross-subsidies among plans provides evidence that ERISA insurance is merely a mechanism to transfer money to a small segment of pension participants. If the insurance truly exists because of so-called market imperfections in the pension industry, the insurance should survive even though risk-related premiums are charged.

If support for ERISA exists only for the purpose of transferring moneys among plans, presumably the support for ERISA insurance will evaporate in the face of an economic premium structure. Not only would a risk-related premium structure make ERISA more efficient but it would provide a litmus test for the underlying support of this aspect of ERISA itself.

Role of Government in Enforcing Long-Term Contracts

An Introduction to the Issues

The above discussion led to proposals that private pensions should be largely unregulated. But even in a free market, the courts and the government have involved themselves in enforcing contracts between private parties. This has been a paramount issue in the pension area, especially since the enactment of ERISA. What role should the government play in enforcing pension contracts?

Before addressing this question, it is instructive to ask first, What contract enforcement policy is currently being followed? It is apparent from the discussion in earlier sections that the policy is more akin to a contract-writing policy than to a pure enforcement policy. But perhaps more importantly, the policy that the government enforces is schizophrenic and elusive.

Pension contract policy is schizophrenic because different policies apply to different pension plans. For defined-contribution plans, subject only to vesting, the pension trust is irrevocable and fully indexed (to market performance). Thus, once firms make contributions to these plans (and vesting occurs) the funds cannot be reclaimed; further, if workers leave the firm, they take full ownership of their accounts with them: no portion reverts to the firm.

The policy for defined-benefit plans differs from that for defined-contribution plans and differs amongst defined-benefit plans. In the general case, the defined-benefit trust fund is irrevocable up to *legal* liabilities incurred (see below). Trust assets beyond this level are revocable to the firm if a termination occurs; without a termination, the "excess" assets are irrevocable. Moreover, for multiemployer plans,[25] all trust assets are irrevocable even upon termination.[26]

Pension policy is elusive because it varies widely as a function of economic forces which are exogenous to pension plans and pension plan sponsors. Consider the case of single employer defined-benefit plans. In these plans, assets that are irrevocable upon termination are not well defined because the definition of irrevocability essentially depends on the inflation rate. When the inflation rate is low, workers are entitled to virtually all assets in the trust fund, even if termination occurs. When the inflation rate is high, large portions of the trust fund may revert to the firm. For example, over the period 1979–1985, $8 billion in reversions were taken by stockholders in these terminations.[27] Who owns the assets in the fund—workers or stockholders—depends on the inflation rate. Why should workers' real claim to pension assets depend on the inflation rate?[28]

A brief discussion of a formal model of the pension contract will crystallize these issues and form the groundwork for discussion of optimal contract-enforcement policy. It is impossible to rationalize a contract-enforcement policy without knowing first which pension contract implicitly has been signed by

---

[25]So-called Taft-Hartley plans are union plans contributed to by many firms (mineworkers, truckers, etc.); the plans are jointly administered by the union and contributing firms.

[26]The irrevocability provision is found in the Taft-Hartley Act.

[27]In 1984, defined-benefit plans held approximately $700 billion in assets. Reversion data is taken from unpublished data from the Pensions Benefit Guaranty Corporation.

[28]These issues arise in pension plan terminations. Recently as high expected inflation has reduced the portion of assets belonging to workers, some firms have terminated plans and either have, or have not, offset consequent worker losses. In the first case, the firm in effect has borrowed moneys from the pension plan while preserving the pension promise; in the second case, the firm has distributed "excess" trust money to stockholders, imposing large capital losses on workers.

firms and workers. It will become apparent that there is little relationship between the *implicit* pension contract struck by workers and firms and the *legal* pension contract enforced by the government. Moreover, the relationship between the two concepts has varied greatly over the postwar period.

The Implicit Pension Contract

The defined-benefit pension contract is essentially built on trust between the firm and worker, in effect involving an agreement that can extend over a period of 50 years of work and retirement. What is the nature of this contract? What do firms really promise workers? Do workers save for their pensions under the assumption that the firm will terminate their plan anytime? Or do they have an implicit contract with the firm that the firm will not terminate the plan, even though the firm has a legal right to do so?

Space precludes a detailed treatment of the implicit-pension contract. But a crude treatment is possible with the use of a deliberately oversimplified model. Suppose an individual starts work with a firm at age zero and expects to retire at age R; at retirement his defined-benefit plan is paid in a lump sum P. If P is determined by wage W, service a (equal to R at retirement) and some constant b, how is P valued by a worker age a? It depends on how the worker views the pension contract.

If the worker takes a strict legal view, he believes the firm will take advantage of its legal right to terminate the plan anytime. In this case, the value of P at age (and service level) a is

$$P_a{}^* = baW_a e^{-i(R-a)} \tag{1}$$

where W_a is the worker's *current* wage at age a, and i is the nominal long-term interest rate. In this case, the value $P_a{}^*$ is the termination value of the pension.

Suppose, however, that while the firm legally could terminate the plan immediately, workers believe they have an *implicit contract* with the firm that the firm will not terminate the plan (except when rare financial exigencies occur), that instead the firm will keep the plan intact and pay workers' pensions at retirement that are proportional to wage at retirement W_R. In this case, the value of P_a at age a is

$$P_a = baW_Re^{-i(R-a)}. \tag{2}$$

The ongoing pension value P_a exceeds the termination value $P_a{}^*$ because wage at retirement W_R exceeds current wage W_a. For example, consider the plausible case where wage growth equals the interest rate. Then the ongoing pension value can be rewritten in terms of current wage:

$$P_a = baW_a. \tag{3}$$

Comparing Expression 3 to Expression 1, it is apparent that the real pension P_a greatly exceeds the legal pension $P_a{}^*$; moreover, the higher the nominal interest rate, the greater is the difference between $P_a{}^*$ and P_a.

If workers pay for their pension through forgone cash wages—and competition amongst firms in the labor and product markets ensure that they must—the amount of wages they forgo depends on whether the pension is a legal contract or an implicit contract. If workers believe they have an implicit contract with the firm to keep the plan intact then, as of age a, they will have forgone wages equal to P_a; if they fear the firm will terminate the plan anytime as it legally could, they would have forgone wages equal to $P_a{}^*$. Workers surely will not contribute the amount equivalent to an undiscounted pension P_a if they expect to receive a discounted pension $P_a{}^*$.

The true nature of this contract has been the target of considerable research. While space considerations preclude a detailed discussion of this research, the results are consistent with the notion that the pension is an implicit long-term contract between workers and firms.[29] There is therefore a great deal of difference between implicit-pension contracts actually struck

[29] See, for example, Ippolito, *Pension, Economics and Public Policy*, chap. 3. In this volume, implications of pension contracts for wage profiles are specified and tested. The results are consistent with the implicit-contract theory and inconsistent with the legal theory. In addition, several studies have shown that pensions deter mobility, a result consistent with the implicit-contract theory and inconsistent with a legal theory. See, for example, B. McCormick and G. Hughes, "The Influence of Pensions on Job Mobility," *Journal of Public Economics* 23 (February 1984), pp. 183–206.

by workers and firms and legal contracts enforced by the government.

Description of Current Pension Policy

Portion of Assets Revocable to the Firm. Workers expect and therefore pay for real pensions. But *legally* the firm can pay workers nominal pensions. What implications does this have for pension contract enforcement?

First, consider the portion of assets which are legally revocable to the firm. Denote real pension liabilities as P and termination pension liabilities as P^*. Legally, firms can terminate the plan anytime, and hence pay nominal P^*, not indexed pensions P. Thus if pension assets are denoted by A, the portion which is revocable, say R/A, is

$$R/A = (A - P^*)/A = 1 - (1/LF) \tag{4}$$

where LF is the legal pension funding ratio. Since legal pension liabilities P^* fall with higher inflation, the portion of assets revocable to the firm can increase dramatically and unexpectedly.

The Firm's Ability to Borrow from the Pension Plan. Now consider the portion of assets and liabilities that the firm can effectively borrow. In particular, consider a firm that has revocable assets in the amount R in the pension fund.

If the firm terminates the plan and makes appropriate arrangements to offset worker losses—what might be termed a pseudo termination[30]—the sole effect of the transaction is that the firm explicitly borrows the amount B^* which is equal to the amount of revocable assets R. The portion of pension assets borrowed B^*/A is

$$B^*/A = (A - P^*)/A = 1 - (1/LF) = R/A. \tag{5}$$

If the inflation rate is sufficiently high, the portion of assets which is revocable, and hence borrowable, can approach 100

[30]The firm can effect a pseudo-termination in numerous ways. One popular way is to terminate the plan and reestablish a similar plan immediately, which awards past service credit and is integrated with the old plan.

percent. Clearly a psuedo-termination effectively permits the firm to borrow moneys far in excess of 10 percent of plan assets.

Moreover, the borrowing constraint is in general a vacuous concept. Since firms promise pensions P but hold only assets A in the pension plan, the amount of pension promises not funded $(P-A)$ is an implicit firm bond held by the pension plan. Hence, the general description of implicit borrowing by the firm in terms of true pension liabilities B/P is

$$B/P = (P - A)/P = 1 - EF \tag{6}$$

where EF is the economic funding ratio: By underfunding the pension plan, the firm finds another way to borrow moneys that can greatly exceed 10 percent of plan assets.

While the IRS enforces a funding policy of sorts, it is clearly nonbinding. The distribution of funding ratios for the (typical) years 1978 and 1981 are shown in Table 4–2. In 1981, for example, approximately one fifth of all liabilities were found in plans less than 50 percent funded; almost one fifth of all liabilities were in plans more than 100 percent funded. These differences cannot be explained by age of plan or other firm and in-

Table 4–2

Economic Funding Ratios in Private Defined-Benefit Pension Plans

	1978		*1981*	
Funding Ratio	*Number of Plans*	*Percent Total Liabilities*	*Number of Plans*	*Percent Total Liabilities*
Less than 25%	216	8%	60	1%
25%–49%	960	23	544	18
50%–74%	1,012	43	1,102	29
75%–99%	634	23	1,202	35
100% or more	342	3	1,115	17
Total	3,164	100%	4,023	100%
Average funding ratio*	.655		.768	

*Overall funding ratios are weighted by pension liabilities in the plan. Active vested liabilities are discounted at 1 percent; current retiree liabilities, at 1.5 percent plus 50 percent of expected inflation.

Source: Data is from a random sample of pension plan annual reports submitted to the Department of Labor in 1978 and 1981. Derivation of economic funding ratio algorithm is found in Richard A. Ippolito, *Pensions, Economics and Public Policy* (Homewood, Ill.: Dow Jones-Irwin, A Pension Research Council monograph, 1986).

dustry attributes:[31] plan sponsors apparently can attain the funding ratios they prefer under current guidelines.[32]

Workers' Claim on Pension Assets. If borrowing policy is not well defined, neither are workers' claims to pension assets. Consider a true termination, that is, one where the firm does not offset worker losses in a new plan. In this case, the firm imposes large capital losses on workers. When a termination occurs, the firm pays off only a portion of true pension promises. In particular, they pay nominal liabilities P^*, not real liabilities P; thus, upon termination, workers keep the portion of real benefits denoted by I^*:

$$I^* = P^*/P. \tag{7}$$

Pension insurance guarantees that the portion of benefits approximately equal to I^* is available to workers upon termination (through the Pension Benefit Guaranty Corporation). Clearly, as inflation increases, the portion ($I^* = P^*/P$) falls because legal pension liabilities fall relative to real liabilities. The portion of workers' real benefits preserved by termination is variable, determined largely by exogenous forces, especially inflation.

Variability of Public Policy. These expressions make it apparent that:

- The amount of irrevocable assets in the pension plan;
- The amount that in effect may be borrowed from the plan;
- The portion of real benefits preserved upon termination; and
- The portion of benefits insured

are all variable concepts that essentially depend on the inflation rate which is exogenous to firms and participants in the pension market. Moreover, the data show that there is no effec-

---

[31] Adjusting for age of plan, size, profitability, and many other plan, firm and industry characteristics cannot explain more than 25 percent of the observed variability in funding ratios. See Ippolito, *Pension, Economics and Public Policy*, chap. 11.

[32] Legal funding ratios usually do not fall significantly below unity.

tive public policy pursued with respect to borrowing: a large portion of firms borrow more than 50 percent of benefit promises within the current system.

The implications of inflation for the pension contract enforced by the federal government are shown in Figures 4–1 and 4–2 for the years 1950 through 1983. Figure 4–1 displays the portion of assets revocable to the typical pension firm *R/A* over the period 1950–1984 and the portion of real benefits preserved upon termination *P*/P* (also the approximate amount insured since 1974). Through the mid–1960s, the portion of assets revocable to the typical pension firm was virtually zero; since 1980, the portion has exceeded 40 percent. The portion of benefits paid upon termination of a typical pension firm *P*/P*—and the

Figure 4–1
Economic and Legal Pension Concepts: 1950–1983

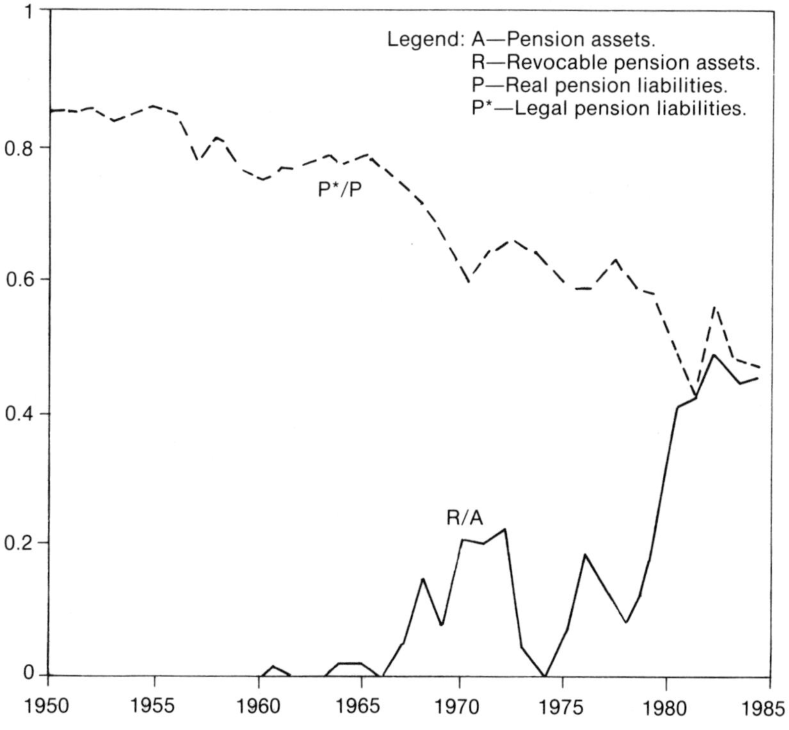

Figure 4–2
Legal and Economic Funding Ratios: 1950–1983

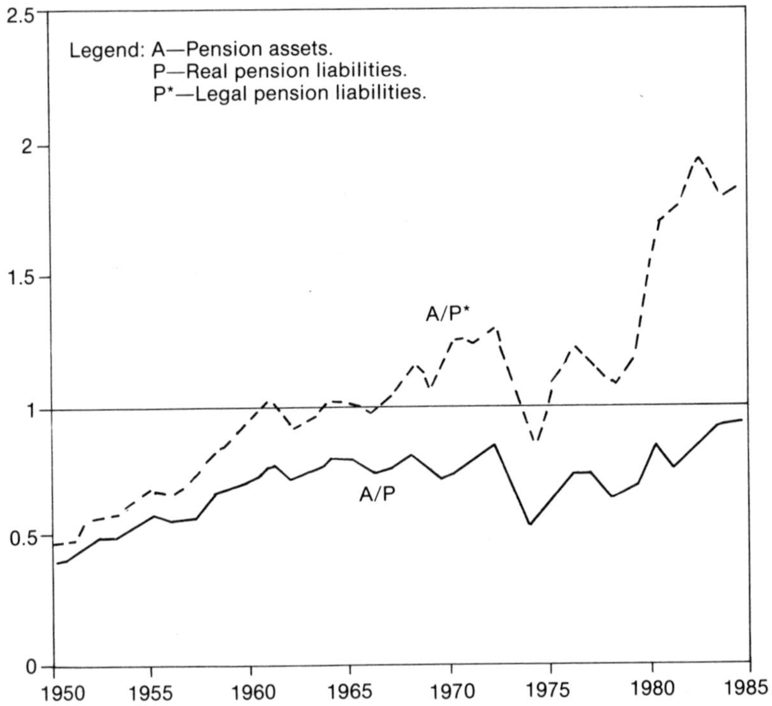

approximate portion insured since 1974—were 75 percent in 1960, 59 percent in 1975, and 44 percent in 1981.[33]

The divergence between economic and legal pension concepts over this period is depicted in Figure 4–2. The economic funding ratio—the portion of *real* benefits held in pension trust (including revocable assets)—is relatively stable over the period (see the schedule labeled A/P in the figure). The legal funding ratio—the portion of *legal* benefits held in trust—is more vari-

[33]The portion insured may be less than P^*/P due to the five-year phase-in of insurance coverage and the limitation on amount of monthly benefits. See Richard A. Ippolito,"Issues Surrounding Pension Plan Terminations," U.S. Department of Labor, mimeo, 1985.

able (see the schedule labeled A/P* in the figure). Through the mid-1960s, the differences between the economic and legal concepts were small. But with the advent of significant inflation beginning in the late 1960s, the differences have become very large, as evinced by the growing spread between the two funding ratios over time.

What Contract Should the Government Enforce?

The above exercise makes it apparent that there are no meaningful trust rules in effect: current policy is elusive and therefore uncertain, leaving property rights vaguely defined. Workers would appear to have a difficult time knowing which assets are revocable and which are not. Moreover, attempts by firms to write either irrevocable or indexed pension contracts are not enforceable: they are superseded by the firm's legal right (especially in nonunion plans) to unilaterally alter any such provision in the contract anytime.[34] This state of confusion needs to be addressed.

Evidence from an Unregulated Market. Having said this, it is in a sense fortuitous that we had the opportunity to view the pension market shock posed by high nominal interest rates (and good stock market performance) in the late 1970s and early 1980s. The terminations for reversion that occurred provide important information about the way an unregulated pension system would work.

First, while approximately $200 billion in legal excess assets existed in 1984,[35] and while the vast majority of firms had legal excess assets in their plans, only $8 billion was actually reclaimed during the period 1979–1985. Second, had all defined-benefit plans unilaterally terminated, almost $400 billion in real expected pension benefits could have been legally canceled

---

[34]That is, even if the firm writes an irrevocable clause in the pension contract, since it is a unilateral contract in the eyes of the law, ERISA clearly permits firms to alter this change at will: it is an unenforceable contract clause.

[35]These data are found in Ippolito, *Pensions, Economics and Public Policy*, chap. 13.

through termination.[36] Yet, only a tiny fraction of this amount was actually canceled.[37]

Despite no government constraints, and despite an opportunity to revert large portions of pension assets to the firm and to impose large capital losses on workers during the post-ERISA period, the private pension system remained almost wholly intact. This is not attributable to government regulation; rather it is a testament to the strength of market forces in the labor markets to enforce long-term implicit contracts.

Underlying Assumptions Underpinning ERISA. It is plausible that in the absence of ERISA—in the absence of any rules about funding, borrowing, and irrevocability—firms and workers may wish to use the pension fund for reasons other than to pay pensions. Put another way, workers and the firm may agree that, under some conditons, it may be optimal to either discontinue the pension fund (notwithstanding legal excess assets in the plan) or to reduce funding levels.[38]

ERISA policy is predicated on the assumption that pension funds serve no productive purposes; that they are the equivalent of savings accounts for workers. If this presumption is correct, it is easy to formulate the optimal policy:

- Make all pension plan trusts irrevocable and require full funding policies.
- Permit terminations anytime but do not permit pension assets to revert to the firm unless assets exceed real liabilities.
- Redefine pension insurance as a percentage of real liabilities.

---

[36]Ibid.

[37]Most large terminations (involving as much as 75 percent of the reversions) occurred in situations where the firm at least attempted to reduce and oftentimes eliminated worker losses. Many if not most terminations for reversion apparently are motivated by the firm's inclination to access moneys in the plan, not to break the implicit pension contract. Moreover, the evidence suggests that many terminations involving substantial worker losses may be attributable to firm failure problems, suggesting the reversion and indeed the entire pension capital loss (P–P^*) may in effect have been given to the firm by workers to participate in the firm's revival. See Ippolito, *Pensions, Economics, and Public Policy*.

[38]A case has been made elsewhere that some firms and workers may find it optimal to keep funding levels low *ad infinitum*. For example, consider the proposition that underfunding may serve to discipline behavior by unionized employees. See Ippolito, *Pensions, Economics and Public Policy*, chaps. 10 and 11.

This would create a well-defined pension contract, one that workers could depend on to provide meaningful retirement income.

This policy, however, is almost surely predicated on a false interpretation of the pension contract. Undoubtedly, workers expect that, under most circumstances, they will receive an indexed pension upon retirement. But they may find it imprudent to enter into a long-term contract with a firm that offers no flexibility to management to take necessary steps to ensure the firm's competitiveness in the long run. They may willingly enter into contracts giving firms flexibility to borrow from the plan, to maintain low funding levels, and to terminate the plan.[39] It would appear unproductive to replace these market contracts with a rigid contract that the government thinks should prevail everywhere.

Government's Role in a Free Pension Market. Competition among firms will ensure that optimal pension contracts are written. If some firms do not find it optimal to use the pension for any reason other than a savings account, they can offer defined-contribution plans. These plans are (in effect) portable and unconditionally irrevocable; and they provide essentially the same tax advantages as defined-benefit plans. Moreover, they can be arranged in ways that offer the annuity and insurance benefits of defined-benefit plans.[40]

The evidence in Table 4–3 offers some encouragement to the notion that markets react to disruption. Defined-contribution plans, as primary plans, represented fewer than 13 percent of workers between 1953 and 1967. But from 1967 to 1981, a period fraught with inflation and accompanying disruption in property rights definitions in defined-benefit plans and growing pension regulation, the percentage increased to 18. More-

---

[39]One function of an underfunded pension plan, for example, might be to bond a union work force—to give it a stake in the long-run viability of the firm. This theory has been developed and tested elsewhere. See Ippolito, *Pensions, Economics and Public Policy*, chaps. 10 and 11.

[40]A model for this option is the plan for university employees, TIAA–CREF, which forces participants to accept annuities (no lump sums)—hence eliminates the classic selectivity problem facing retirees with lump sums—and which spreads investment losses or gains in the portfolios across cohorts.

over, workers and firms evinced a tendency toward diversification in their pension plan; by 1981, fully one third of workers in primary defined-benefit plans had secondary defined-contribution plans in the same firm. If nothing else, these numbers dispel the notion that the pension market is lethargic, that it cannot change its character in response to market and regulatory conditions.

If residual concern remains that competition amongst firms will not generate optimal pensions, the availability of unlimited IRAs would solve this problem. Intensive competition amongst firms offering different types of plans and IRAs makes it increasingly unlikely that workers will make decisions without understanding the opportunity costs of defined-benefit pensions. Workers can plainly see their tax-preferred IRA option which in turn will force firms to make their plans competitive. Moreover, with substantially eliminated pension regulation, firms will have more freedom to structure pensions tailored to firms' needs and workers' preferences.

Given competition among firms, and the availability of defined-contribution plans and unlimited IRAs, the only defined-benefit pensions left would be those that offered substantial productivity gains. Since individuals have unlimited

Table 4–3

Percent of Participants with Defined-Contribution Plan Coverage, 1947–1981 (selected years)

Year	*(1) Participants with DC-Plan Primary Coverage*	*(2) DB-Plan Participants with DC-Plan Secondary Coverage**
1947	18.6%	5.7%
1953	12.0	12.6
1960	12.2	20.6
1967	12.9	20.9
1974	14.6	23.7
1981	18.0	33.0

*The notation DC means defined contribution; DB means defined benefit.

Source: Richard A. Ippolito, *Pensions, Economics, and Public Policy* (Homewood, Ill.: Dow Jones-Irwin, A Pension Research Council monograph, 1986), chap. 6.

IRAs available in a free market, it can be concluded that any participation in a firm's pension contract would be voluntary: No regulation of that contract is required. If workers want assurance that some portion of promised benefits will be paid, presumably they will require firms to find insurance in the private market.

Under a free-market policy, the government does not need to concern itself with which pension contract is the right one. The market determines this. The government extricates itself from the contract-writing business, and restricts itself instead to the contract-enforcement business. Three actions by the government would be consistent with this policy:

- Legislation should be enacted making irrevocability language legally binding on the firm and bankruptcy courts: if the firm chooses to use the specified language, workers would be assured that portions of assets designated as irrevocable would indeed be irrevocable.
- Full disclosure of all relevant economic aspects of the plan should be required, including revocability provisions, insurance levels, and full consequences of termination for real benefit levels.
- A reversion tax should be assessed on all reversions to the firm. This tax—equal to the tax advantages embodied in the pension trust—ensures that firms will not use the pension plan as a corporate savings account.

Given these conditions and the availability of unlimited IRAs, the formal regulatory system could be substantially eliminated. Courts will enforce the stated contract provisions; insurance companies will enforce appropriate fiduciary requirements; and the IRS would continue to monitor pension plans for tax abuse. Otherwise, the system would operate in a free market.

Conclusions and Summary of Policy Recommendations

National public policy toward pensions should reflect the principles of free choice among the nation's citizenry. The federal government should arrange its tax and regulatory policies in ways that neutralize the government's role in deciding which kinds of pensions workers should have, when they should retire, how much they should save, and the like. Under an efficient national pension policy—one characterized by unlimited IRAs and unregulated pensions—a large amount of competition would emerge, generating more choice for workers among retirement savings plans. The tie between firms and pension savings would be broken except for those workers whose coverage under firm pensions would substantially augment their long-term productivity. The government's role would be reduced to one of enforcing, not writing pension contracts.

The federal government has followed an enlightened pension policy in the tax area. Despite enforcing a comprehensive income tax policy which heavily taxes and hence discourages nonpension savings, tax policy toward pensions has reflected expenditure-tax principles: Public tax policy has not distorted individual choice to save for retirement. This policy has not only removed potentially large distortions in retirement ages and retirement consumption, but has no doubt reduced pressure on public pension and old age welfare programs.

While the government's overall pension tax policy has been efficient, its regulatory policy has erected a myriad of troubling, unproductive restrictions on individual choice. The centerpiece of a policy that frees the market of these intrusions is the elimination of the limits on Individual Retirement Accounts. Once this option is made available to workers, firm pensions can be freed from most regulation. Pensions will survive only if they serve a productive purpose in the firm.

A summary list of policy recommendations is now given, accompanied by Table 4–4, which succinctly presents prescriptions for an efficient retirement system.

- *Retain the tax deferral treatment of pension savings.* Current tax treatment of pensions essentially mimics an expenditure-tax structure, thereby reducing potentially large distortions in workers' choice of retirement age and retirement consumption. Moreover, by pursuing such tax policy, it is likely that pressure on public pensions and welfare systems has been substantially reduced.
- *Tax Social Security contributions and benefits in the same*

way that private pensions are treated. By altering the tax treatment of Social Security to conform to the treatment of private pensions, all savings for retirement will be made through vehicles that foster neutrality between current and future consumption. Individuals will no longer be biased by the income tax code to favor a combination of private and public systems even though one alone might be preferred otherwise.[41]

- *Eliminate all limits on Individual Retirement Accounts.* This change makes IRAs fully competitive with private pensions. Such a provision (together with the corporate pension tax deduction) ensures that private pensions would survive in the long run if either significant efficiency gains are generated by deferred-wage schemes or annuity rates are reduced substantially by mandatory group participation. Otherwise, pensions will be replaced by IRAs.[42]
- *Deregulate private pension plans.* Given the availability of unconstrained IRAs and defined-contribution plans, individuals would have access to favorable tax treatment without joining private defined-benefit pensions. It therefore can be presumed that private pensions, together with their attendant rules, will persist only if they stimulate substantial productivity or other efficiency effects. Rules that stem from various Revenue Acts or ERISA regulations which constrain pension plan rules—rules that deter mobility or induce retirement at particular ages,[43] or create stylized plans for particular groups in the firm or permit variable savings rates—should be eliminated.[44]
- *Transfer federal pension insurance to the private sector.* The federal government can mandate insurance coverage (at current levels) in the private market, providing reinsurance

[41]Such changes were put into effect in 1984 but are limited in their impact to a small portion of the retiree population; this policy should be applied equally to all Social Security recipients.

[42]The introduction of salary reduction 401(k) plans in 1981 is not a perfect substitute for the expansion of IRAs but nonetheless represents a significant step toward introducing more flexibility into the private pension system.

[43]Again, 401(k) plans represent a positive step in introducing more flexibility into the pension system but do not yield the free-market solution described in this chapter.

[44]At the same time, the actuarial penalties to work past age 65 enforced by the Social Security system should be removed immediately, not in the year 2010, as currently scheduled.

Table 4–4
Prescriptions for Efficient Retirement Policy

Policy	*Current Policy*	*Recommended Policy*
Social Security system		
1. Taxation of benefits	Include one half of benefits as taxable income if retirement income exceeds $32,000 (for a married couple).	Include one half of benefits as taxable income.
2. Earnings test	Lose 50 cents of benefits for each dollar of annual income over approximately $7,000 until age 70.	Eliminate.
Pension tax policy		
1. Corporate level	Pension contributions deductible.	Retain.
2. Pension trust	Tax exempt.	Retain.
3. Income tax	Pension benefits included as taxable income during retirement.	Retain.
4. Defined benefit limits	Cannot fund for annual benefits in excess of $90,000.	Eliminate or substantially increase.
Individual Retirement Accounts		
1. Tax policy	Same as pensions.	Retain.
2. Limits	$2,000 annual contribution.	Eliminate (or make equivalent to pensions).*
Pension plan regulation		
1. IRS discrimination rules	Require similar pensions for all workers within the firm.	Eliminate.
2. ERISA constraints on pension rules	Participation, backloading, vesting, and nonforfeiture rules for all plans.	Eliminate.
3. ERISA fiduciary rules	Operate pension plans as an independent trust.	Retain.†
4. Rules regulating retirement age	No rules.	Retain.
Other pension plans		
1. 401(k) plans	Allow combined contributions up to 25 percent of salary.	Retain.
2. Cafeteria plans	Allow workers to shift contributions among welfare and 401(k) plans.	Retain.

*This policy may require elimination or limitation of deductibility of interest on borrowed moneys.
†This does not mean some specific rules might not be modified.

Table 4–4 *(concluded)*

Policy	*Current Policy*	*Recommended Policy*
ERISA insurance	Publicly operated by the PBGC.	Voluntary insurance from private insurance companies at market premiums. (If mandatory insurance is retained, the insurance should still be transferred to the private sector, and the insurance level should be redefined as a percent of real benefits).
Contract enforcement	Different revocability provisions for different pension plans; revocable assets and workers' claims to real benefits defined by exogenous factors; ineffective borrowing and funding policy.	Second-best solution: establish firm revocability rules independent of exogenous forces, introducing certainty to workers about which portion of assets they own. Establish a borrowing policy in terms of real pension benefits recognizing underfunding as borrowing. First best solution: permit flexibility in the pension contract in borrowing, funding, termination, and insurance provisions: the government requires full disclosure, enables firms to establish binding irrevocability provisions in plans, and establishes a reversion tax upon termination.

to rule out solvency problems in the face of catastrophic temporal events. The private market will establish economic premium structures which will include the institution of risk-related premiums. The establishment of this scheme will provide a litmus test for the legitimate support of ERISA.

- *Second-best solution: Establish coherent pension contract policy.* Under present law, trust revocability provisions differ among pension plans and are randomly affected by inflation and investment market performace. As a second-best solution, the rules should be defined in a meaningful way. The portion of trust assets which are revocable should be defined in terms of real pension liabilities, providing certainty about who owns which portion of pension assets. Borrowing constraints should be written in terms of real pension benefits, recognizing underfunding as an explicit firm bond.
- *First-best solution: Enforce free-market contracts.* In conjunction with the availability of unlimited IRAs and pension deregulation, the government should withdraw from the contract-writing business and constrain itself instead to the contract-enforcement business. Flexibility in revocability, borrowing, funding, and insurance provisions should be permitted. In conjunction with this policy, full disclosure of the pension contract should be required and the government should enable firms to enforce irrevocability provisions and establish a reversion tax upon termination.

Appendix

Impact of the Tax Policy on Size of the Pension Plan System

In this appendix, the implications of pension tax policy for past and projected growth of private pensions is briefly stated. Tax policy toward pension plans not only eliminates the double tax on savings; it offers workers an opportunity to defer taxation on savings, thereby affording them an opportunity to smooth income. Given the progressive tax scheme in the United States, these privileges make pension plans a highly tax-preferred vehicle for long-term savings. Though individual retirement accounts (IRAs) have been offered in limited amounts since 1974, these tax advantages have typically been made available only through pension plans offered through firms.

It is inconceivable that the size of the current private system is not largely attributable to the special pension tax provisions in the U.S. tax code and the accompanying high marginal tax rates which have prevailed in the code since World War II. These advantages can easily account for 20 to 40 percent of retirees' private pension income.[45] Thus, a plausible and perhaps compelling proposition is that pension tax policy and the high marginal tax rates in the U.S. tax structure are largely responsible for the creation of the pension system. Available evidence lends strong support to this notion.[46]

Data presented in Table 4–5 illustrates the implications of pension growth after World War II. Consider the numbers in column 1. In 1950, private and public pensions held $66 billion (1984 dollars), in 1981 they held $1 trillion (1984 dollars), and by the year 2000 they will hold almost $3 trillion (1984 dollars).

Some additional pension calculations are presented in the table. These numbers express pension assets per worker (including all covered and uncovered workers in the private and public sectors) and as a fraction of total wages paid. These data show that in the year 2000, real pension assets per worker will be 14 times greater than they were in the year 1950 (see columns 2 and 3). Most of this growth has already taken place, increasing by a factor of seven over the period 1950–1981. But it will still double again by the year 2000.

As a percentage of national wages, pension assets will grow by a factor of eight over the period 1950–2000 (see columns 4 and 5). They grew by a factor of 5.5 from 1950 until 1981, but they will increase by an additional 50 percent by the year 2000. Put another way, over the 50-year period, real pension assets will have grown at a rate approximately two-and-one-half times the rate of expansion of the economy as a whole, measured by employment income (7.5 percent per year versus 3.0 percent).

Regardless of the measure used, it is apparent that the spread of pensions throughout the work force and the economy has

---

[45]See Ippolito, *Pensions, Economics and Public Policy*, chap. 2.

[46]Cross-section evidence shows that high-income (high-tax) workers have a much higher probability of pension coverage; time-series evidence is consistent with the notion that the erection of a widespread income tax structure with high marginal tax rates led to the post–World War II growth of the pension industry. See Ippolito, *Pensions, Economics and Public Policy*, chap. 2.

Table 4–5

Pension Assets in Relation to Employment and Wages, 1950–2000[1]

Year	(1) Pension Assets ($1984 billion)	Pension Assets per Worker[2] (2) 1984 Dollars	(3) Indexed to 1981	Pension Assets as a Fraction of Total Wages[3] (4) Ratio	(5) Indexed to 1981
1950	$ 66	$ 1,523	.14	.13	.18
1955	137	2,831	.26	.22	.29
1960	185	4,327	.40	.31	.41
1965	427	6,383	.58	.41	.54
1970	548	6,981	.64	.44	.58
1975	658	8,651	.79	.55	.74
1981	1,062	10,907	1.00	.75	1.00
1990	1,702*	14,699*	1.35*	.87*	1.16*
2000	2,879*	21,429*	1.96*	1.14*	1.51*

[1]Includes private plus public pension plans.

[2]The work force is comprised of the nonagricultural private and public work force; it is assumed to grow at a 1.7 percent rate after 1981.

[3]The real wage rate is the nonagricultural private sector weekly wage times 52 adjusted to 1984 dollars; it is assumed to grow at the rate of 1.1 percent after 1981.

*Denotes projected value.

Source: Richard A. Ippolito. *Pension Economics and Public Policy* (Homewood, Ill.: Dow Jones-Irwin, Pension Research Council monograph. 1986), chap. 7.

been dramatic since World War II and will continue to be impressive until at least the turn of the century.

Over a period of 30 years, labor markets have moved from a situation where a small portion of the work force retired with a pension to one where two thirds of workers will receive a pension, including virtually all middle- and upper-bracket wage earners. Moreover, these pensions have become more generous and are being supplemented more often by secondary plans (33 percent of pension-covered workers have secondary, usually defined-contribution, pension plans). The improvements in coverage and benefit amounts are succinctly summarized in column 4 of the table. In 1981, pension assets were 75 percent of wages paid in the United States in that year; in 1950, they were 13 percent of wages; by the year 2000, pension assets will be 114 percent of wages. All of this means that pensions will continue to represent an important source of retirement for workers. It is estimated that two thirds of the current work force will retire with a pension; on average, the first year annuity was $6,300 in 1984, 23 percent of the final wage.[47]

[47]Ibid., Table 1–1.

5

Social Security: Past, Present, and Future

by C. Arthur Williams, Jr.*

On August 14, 1985, Old-Age, Survivors, Disability, and Health Insurance, popularly known as Social Security and Medicare, celebrated its 50th birthday. The event received first-page, cover-story, and prime-time attention in the media. Given the unique, tremendously important contribution of this Social Security program toward our individual and collective economic security, this attention was well deserved.

At least two special surveys were conducted to determine the degree of public satisfaction with the program on its 50th birthday and their confidence in its future. According to a study conducted by Yankelovich, Skelly, and White, commissioned by the American Association of Retired Persons, 85 to 90 percent of all Americans opposed discontinuing the program and replacing it with reliance on private pension plans. About 73 percent of the nonretired population said they would stay in the Social Security system even if they were not forced to do

*Professor, University of Minnesota. The author appreciates Robert J. Myers' review for technical accuracy.

so.[1] The second study, conducted for *U.S. News & World Report* by Civic Service, Inc., indicated that 38 percent had no confidence that they would receive their Social Security benefits. Only 23 percent were very confident. On the other hand, about 44 percent expect Social Security benefits, if paid, to provide half or more of their retirement income.[2]

The facts suggest that Social Security does face some serious problems and some very significant changes. For example, Hospital Insurance faces short- and long-run financing problems. The OASDI system is in much better financial shape, but after the turn of the century it too may face another financial crisis. In addition, the basic role and structure of Social Security is being increasingly questioned. Some persons have recommended that the welfare aspects of Social Security be separated from the insurance portion. Others have advocated that benefits be limited to those who satisfy a means test. Many have urged that OASDHI be revised substantially to reflect the many economic, demographic, and social changes that have already occurred in our nation since Social Security was born and others that are likely to occur in the future.

The purpose of this chapter is to trace briefly the history of Social Security, examine the basic principles upon which it has been based, and comment on its future.[3] That future may witness revolutionary or evolutionary changes, depending upon many factors. This chapter will describe briefly some of the revolutionary and evolutionary changes that have already been proposed.

---

[1]"Study: Social Security Gains Backing," *Journal of Commerce*, August 9, 1985, p. 8A. See also "Opinion Polls Find Wide Support for Social Security, Medicare," *AARP News Bulletin*, September 1985, pp. 1–3.

[2]"Social Security at 50 Faces New Crossroads," *U.S. News & World Report*, August 12, 1985, pp. 40–43.

[3]In preparing this paper the author read or reread many books and articles on Social Security, a large proportion of which are cited in the chapter. Four books not otherwise cited that he consulted frequently were the following: Robert M. Ball, *Social Security Today and Tomorrow* (New York: Columbia University Press, 1978); Robert J. Myers, *Social Security*, 3rd ed. (Homewood, Ill.: Richard D. Irwin, 1985); George E. Rejda, *Social Insurance and Economic Security*, 2nd ed. (Englewood Cliffs, N.J.: Prentice Hall, 1984); and C. A. WIlliams, Jr., J. G. Turnbull, and E. F. Cheit, *Economic and Social Security*, 5th ed. (New York: John Wiley & Sons, 1982).

A Short History

To understand the present status of Social Security and to make intelligent comments about its future, it is important to know how the system originated and developed to the present. This short history will describe the Social Security system at its birth in the midst of the Great Depression and some of the major changes that have occurred since that time.

The Beginning

In 1935, President Franklin D. Roosevelt signed the landmark legislation that established the Social Security system. All workers under age 65 employed in commerce and industry, excluding railroad workers who were covered under a separate federal Railroad Retirement System, were covered. Not covered were self-employed persons; domestic employees; farm laborers; federal, state, and local government employees; employees of charitable, educational, and religious nonprofit organizations; and some other special cases.

Whereas the present system provides retirement, survivorship, disability, and medical expense insurance, the original program was limited to retirement and lump-sum death benefits. Fully retired persons who had worked in covered employment in each of five years after 1936 prior to reaching age 65 and who had accumulated wage credits of $2,000 or more, were entitled to an old-age pension. The monthly pension amount was calculated as follows: ½ percent of the first $3,000 of accumulated wages plus 1/12 percent of the next $42,000 plus 1/24 percent of the next $84,000. Only the first $3,000 per year of each worker's wage was to be taxed and to be counted in the accumulated wage credits. In 1937, however, only about 2 percent of the covered employees had wages exceeding $3,000. The maximum monthly benefit was $85, the minimum $10. If a worker died before he or she had received at least 3.5 percent of his or her taxed wages, the difference was returned to his or her estate. If the worker failed to qualify for monthly benefits at 65, he or she received a lump sum equal to 3.5 percent of the total taxed wages. The first monthly benefits were to be paid in 1942.

The annual taxes, starting in 1937, were 1 percent of the first $3,000 of wages to be paid by the employee and matched by the employer. This contribution was scheduled to increase by 0.5 percent every three years until it reached 3 percent in 1949. This tax schedule would have created a large trust fund, the interest on which would be used to pay a substantial proportion of the costs. For example, by 1980 the interest was expected to equal about 40 percent of the disbursements. However, because the government assumed from the beginning that the system would operate indefinitely into the future, the fund was never intended to be as large as that required by private life insurers for full funding.

Some Major Changes since 1935

Before the first benefits were to be paid, the system was changed significantly. In 1939 the eligibility requirements were liberalized. Workers qualified for benefits based on their quarters of coverage, calendar quarters in which they were paid at least $50 in covered employment. For example, for workers to be fully insured as of any age, they had to have earned two quarters of coverage per elapsed year since January 1, 1937 (or, if later, the beginning of the year in which he or she attained age 22). The maximum requirement was 40 quarters, the minimum 6.

The 1939 amendments also changed the benefit formula. Instead of being a function of total taxable earnings, the benefit now depended upon average taxable earnings. This change greatly increased the benefits for persons approaching retirement age in the near future. The formula also provided higher benefits for workers with lower average taxable earnings (as did also the 1935 formula). The benefit thus became more clearly a floor of protection than a savings program. Further evidence of this shift was the addition of benefits for the wife and children of a retired worker. OAI also became OASI with the establishment of survivorship benefits for widows, children, and dependent parents. Beneficiaries, including a retired worker, were permitted to earn up to $14.99 a month before they would lose their benefits.

Despite the liberalization of the eligibility requirements and the benefits, no change was made in the contribution rate schedule. Many legislators favored a government contribution to the system from general revenues, but Congress took no specific action.

Space does not permit a discussion of all the changes that have taken place since the 1939 amendments but, in order to indicate the importance of these changes, some of the more significant amendments affecting (1) covered employment, (2) insured status, (3) benefits, and (4) financing are described briefly below.

Covered Employment. Originally only 6 out of 10 gainfully employed persons worked in covered employments. In 1950 many new persons were covered under special conditions including nonfarm self-employed persons, farm laborers, domestic workers, employees of state and local governments, and employees of charitable, educational, and religious nonprofit organizations. The fraction of jobs covered rose to about 9 out of 10. Further extensions of coverage resulted from 1954, 1956, and 1965 amendments. The 1983 amendments added the President of the United States, members of Congress, and all new federal government employees, plus all employees of nonprofit organizations who had not been covered by election. The only major group of employees still not covered are those state and local government employees not covered because their governmental unit has not extended coverage to its employees (or those persons who were employed when such coverage was extended but declined to participate) and federal employees under a retirement system who were hired before 1984.

Insured Status. Because so many employees were covered for the first time by the 1950 amendments, these same amendments moved the earliest starting date for determining insured status from January 1, 1937, to January 1, 1951. The 1960 amendments reduced the quarters-of-coverage requirement from two quarters per elapsed year to one and one third. One year later the required quarters of coverage per elapsed year was further reduced to one.

Workers continued to accumulate quarters of coverage by being paid $50 in a calendar quarter in covered employment until 1977, when the requirement was changed (for 1978) to $250 of annual earnings, the maximum number of quarters that could be earned in a calendar year being four. This $250 was to be adjusted each year to reflect increases in average national earnings.

When Disability Insurance was estabished in 1956, to receive benefits, in addition to being fully insured, a worker had to have earned 20 quarters of coverage out of the last 40. In 1967, an alternative requirement was introduced for persons disabled before age 31 to one half the quarters elapsing since the year in which they were age 21 (but not less than 6 quarters of coverage in the last 12 quarters).

Under Hospital Insurance, Part A of Medicare established in 1965, benefits were made payable only to OASDI or Railroad Retirement System beneficiaries aged 65 or over. Other persons aged 65 before 1968 were also eligible, regardless of whether they had ever contributed to the system. As a result of 1972 legislation, disabled OASDI or railroad retirement beneficiaries became eligible for benefits after 24 months on the monthly benefits roll. Furthermore, all aged persons who did not otherwise qualify were permitted to enroll by paying the full cost of coverage. Finally, special coverage was extended to fully or currently insured persons and their dependents or survivors with chronic kidney disease who need transplants or dialysis with kidney machines.

Supplementary Medical Insurance, Part B of Medicare, which relates primarily to physician fees, differs from the other parts of OASDHI in that participation has always been voluntary. Participation, however, has been limited to those covered under Hospital Insurance except that from the beginning all aged persons have been permitted to enroll.

Benefits. Following the important 1939 benefit changes, the benefits remained fairly stable until 1950, when benefits were increased an average of 77 percent to reflect the increase in prices that had occurred during the World War II and the postwar years. In that same year the monthly earnings test limit was raised to $50 and no longed applied to persons aged 75 or over. In computing the worker's average monthly earnings for benefit determinations, some of the lowest earnings years could now be omitted. In 1954 the earnings test limit was increased to $1,200 per year and the age 75 exemption reduced to age 72.

The 1956 amendments permitted women to retire as early as age 62 with actuarially reduced benefits and reduced the age at which widows without children and some others could claim benefits. The earnings test was changed in 1960 so that the beneficiary lost only $1 in benefits for each dollar of earnings in excess of the annual exempt amount. In 1961, men were permitted to retire as early as age 62 with actuarially reduced benefits. Because of 1965 amendments, children beneficiaries who were full-time students could receive benefits until age 22.

The 1972 benefit changes are particularly noteworthy. Following the precedent set in 1950, Congress had from time to time, on an ad hoc basis, increased new benefits and benefits in progress to reflect rising wages and prices. The 1972 amendments increased benefits by 20 percent, which far exceeded the increase in prices since the last ad hoc adjustment. These amendments also introduced automatic increases in the benefits and taxable earnings base to match future increases in prices and wages, respectively. Other important changes made in 1972 included a much higher minimum benefit for long-term workers, a further liberalization of the earnings test, and, for the first time, increased benefits for those who delayed their retirement after age 65.

December 1977 amendments corrected an extremely important technical error in the way in which the initial benefits had been adjusted to reflect price increases during the employee's earning career. The effect was a decrease in these benefits in the future compared with what they otherwise would have been. The 1977 amendments also reduced the earnings test exemption age from age 72 to 70, effective in 1982 (later delayed to 1983). The 1981 amendments ended a small minimum benefit for future eligibles (not the special minimum benefit for long-term workers), eliminated the student benefits granted in 1965, and terminated mothers' and fathers' benefits when the youngest child attains age 16 (unless disabled).

The 1983 amendments made many important changes. For example, the cost-of-living adjustments that were scheduled to be paid for each June were deferred to December. Some beneficiaries were required to include part of their OASDI benefits in their taxable income for income tax purposes. Benefits were liberalized for some groups of divorced and disabled spouses (who, at present, are primarily women). Starting in 1990, the earnings test will be further liberalized, the delayed retirements credit will be gradually increased, and, most important, early in the next century the normal retirement age will increase to age 66 and later 67.

In 1954, OASI became OASDI with the addition of a disability freeze that preserved death and retirement benefits for eligible workers with long-term total disabilities. Income benefits for the worker starting at age 50 were added in 1956, dependents' benefits in 1958, and benefits prior to age 50 in 1960. In 1972, the waiting period before benefits started was reduced from the original six months to five months.

With the establishment of Medicare in 1965, OASDI became OASDHI, its present title. The major benefit changes in these programs have been legislated increases in the Supplementary Medical Insurance annual deductible from $50 to $60 in 1972 (effective in 1978) and $75 in 1981 (effective in 1982), the 1967 transfer of outpatient hospital diagnostic services from HI to SMI, and the 1980 removal of the 100-day limitation on home health services under HI and SMI. Increases in the HI deductibles, which are tied to increases in average daily hospital aggregate costs, have of course also affected benefits, as have changes in the ways the Medicare program pays providers for their services or recognizes their charges.

Financing. As noted earlier, the original Act called for employee contributions that were scheduled to increase gradually to 3 percent in 1949. Congress, however, continually postponed increasing the contribution rate and in 1947 abandoned the schedule. Since that time the maximum taxable earnings and the contribution rates have been increased periodically, but there has always been a long-term schedule of contribution rates in the law, changed from time to time. In 1965 the payroll tax was increased to finance Hospital Insurance benefits, and persons electing coverage under Supplementary Medical Insurance were charged a monthly premium, general revenues being used to pay part of the costs.

The 1972 amendments made significant changes in the contribution schedule. Starting in 1975, the maximum taxable earnings were to be automatically adjusted to match increases in average national wages, instead of on an ad hoc basis. In response to a financial crisis, however, as a result of 1977 amendments, in 1979, 1980, and 1981 this base was raised more than the percentage increases in earnings. The tax rates were also increased significantly.

Interfund borrowing was first authorized in late 1981 and continued by the 1983 amendments (but only until 1989). The 1983 amendments increased only slightly the combined OASDHI employee contribution rates (and then only in 1988–89).

Because the tax increases scheduled for the early years were continually postponed and before benefits in the early years of operations were increased significantly by the 1939 Act, the Trust Fund did not grow nearly as rapidly as had been expected and a larger share of the tax burden was transferred to future generations. The Revenue Act of 1943 authorized congressional appropriations to Social Security, but none were ever made. In 1950, Congress declared that the system should be self-supporting. It adopted a higher contribution schedule and over the next two decades created a combined trust fund that was more than a contingency fund. The 1972 amendments, however, created the present concept. Future contributions plus interest earnings of the trust fund were still supposed to be sufficient to pay all benefits and expenses for the next 75 years, but the contributions were to be scheduled on the basis of less conservative actuarial assumptions than in the past. The program thus moved closer to a pay-as-you-go system, with the Trust Fund serving primarily as a contingency fund. Contribution and benefit changes enacted in 1977 and 1983 became necessary when the system failed to meet this test by a significant amount.

Basic Principles

Throughout its history Social Security has been characterized by certain basic principles. Their interpretation and their strength have varied over time, but they have always been present. These basic principles are: (1) a balance between private equity and social adequacy, (2) benefits based on presumed need, (3) a floor-of-protection objective, (4) a self-supporting system, (5) less than full funding, (6) a contributory system, and (7) an implied intergenerational contract.

Balance between Private Equity and Social Adequacy

One of the most distinctive features of Social Security is the balance it provides between private equity and social adequacy.[4] If the system were based strictly on private equity, benefits would be related actuarially to contributions. Redistribution of income among participants would be limited to those associated with the pooling of risks under an insurance program. No additional redistribution would occur from higher-paid workers to lower-paid workers, from the workers without dependents to those with dependents, or from the workers of the next generation to the workers of the present generation. The only reasons for involving the government in such a scheme would be (1) compulsion and (2) economies of scale. By making the system compulsory, the government can force persons to prepare for the future who might otherwise lack the discipline to do so. This compulsion, coupled with the magnitude of a federal program, should produce economies of scale that would enable the program to minimize the transaction costs associated with the benefits.

A system based solely upon social adequacy would provide all beneficiaries with an "adequate" income or "adequate" medical care. The benefit would be the same, regardless of the worker's prior earnings, but the benefit would vary with the number of dependents. A few foreign social security systems are structured to provide such benefits.

As noted earlier, from the beginning the United States' approach has been a compromise between these two objectives. The original retirement benefit formula would have increased the monthly pension as the worker's accumulated wage credits increased, but not proportionately. Later formulas shifted the

---

[4]See Reinhard A. Hohaus, "Equity, Adequacy, and Related Factors in Old Age Security," *The Record* 37 (American Institute of Actuaries, 1938).

balance more toward social adequacy by including a minimum benefit and altering the bend points and slopes so that the benefit did not increase as rapidly as a function of earnings as it had originally. The addition of retirement, death, and disability benefits that depended upon the presence of dependents was a further step. Yet the system retained an important link to earnings that is consistent with a desire to reward individual efforts and initiative and to reflect differences among families in the standards of living that may be threatened by retirement, death, or disability. Examples of shifts back toward private equity are the scheduled increases in the benefit for delayed retirements, the termination of the minimum benefit except for long-time, low-paid workers, and the elimination of dependent children benefits after age 18 (except for those who are disabled). Thus the balance between social adequacy and private equity has changed over time, but it is still a basic feature of the system.[5]

Benefits Based on Presumed Need

To satisfy the social adequacy objective, the system does not impose a needs test. Instead the benefits are structured on the basis of presumed needs. Lower-paid workers are presumed to need a higher proportion of their earnings replaced than do higher-paid workers; workers with dependents presumably need a higher replacement rate than those without dependents.

The actual needs, however, may not be the same as the presumed needs. For example, some of the lower-paid workers may have other sources of income that reduce their needs substantially. Higher-paid workers may not need the same percentage increase in benefits for their dependents as do lower-paid workers.

The system would cost less if the welfare component of the system provided only means-tested benefits. The program, however, places a higher value on the dignity of the individual

---

[5]Using a fable of Homer, Calvin, and Jack, Richard Musgrave described social insurance as a device to protect a prudent, compassionate majority from the imprudent minority and to hold compassion within suitable limits. Richard A. Musgrave, "The Role of Social Insurance in an Overall Program for Social Welfare," in *The American System of Social Insurance*, ed., William G. Bowen, Frederick H. Harbison, Richard A. Lester, and Herman M. Somers (New York: McGraw-Hill, 1968), chap. 2. See also the discussion by Albert Rees, pp. 41–43.

and avoidance of the stigma associated with a means test. A means test is also expensive to administer.

Floor of Protection Objective

The goal of Social Security, according to most observers, is to provide a floor of protection. What this term means, however, is subject to many interpretations. Clearly, however, as long as the benefits are expected to bear some relationship to earnings, the floor is not supposed to be the same for all otherwise similarly situated individuals and families.

One way to interpret the floor is the minimum standard of living the system should provide for any worker plus how this standard should increase with increasing earnings. Another interpretation is the extent to which the participants are expected to be able to rely exclusively upon Social Security for the protection they need against the covered contingencies. The views range from those who believe that only lower-paid workers (or not even them) should expect to depend solely upon Social Security for retirement, death, and health insurance to those who believe that for most workers Social Security should become the sole source of such support, thus greatly reducing the need for private supplementation.

When President Franklin D. Roosevelt signed the Social Security Act on August 14, 1935, he made the following statement:

> We can never insure 100 percent of the population against 100 percent of the hazards and vicissitudes of life, but we have tried to frame a law which will give some measure of protection to the average citizen and his family against the loss of a job and against poverty-ridden old age.

This statement implies that the protection to be provided, though important, would leave considerable room for private supplementation.[6]

Few attempts have been made to articulate this floor of protection more precisely. For persons who worked full-time during their careers at the federal minimum wage, the 1979 Advisory Council recommended a primary insurance amount

---

[6]*Public Papers and Addresses of Franklin D. Roosevelt, 1935* (Washington, D.C.: U.S. Government Printing Office, 1935).

equal to the poverty level. The Council also agreed that as a worker's earnings rise, the present value of the increase in future benefits should at least equal the present value of the increased taxes that they (not their employers) must pay on additional earnings.[7] For "regular full-time workers at low earnings levels" the 1965 Advisory Council mentioned as a possible goal benefits high enough so that such a worker would not "have to turn to public assistance to meet regular living expenses."[8] Both councils recommended that for higher-paid workers the floor should be higher but not proportionately so. The formulas they proposed would provide much less than the average worker would require to maintain the same standard of living after retirement as before. In other words, private supplementation was expected.[9]

A Self-Supporting System

For the most part, Social Security has been a self-supporting system. The benefits and servicing expenses have been funded by payroll taxes paid by participating employers and employees. This approach, it is argued, places the tax burden on the people who will benefit directly from the system and, by identifying and emphasizing the cost of the benefits, encourages a careful review of proposed liberalizations. Some persons argue, however, that Social Security's contribution to the general welfare justifies at least some contribution from nonearmarked general revenues. They also argue that the income tax, which provides most of the general revenue, is superior to the payroll tax

---

[7]*Reports of the 1979 Advisory Council on Social Security* (Washington, D.C.: 1979).

[8]"Report of the Advisory Council on Social Security: The Status of the Social Security Program and Recommendations for Its Improvement," *Social Security Bulletin* 38, no. 3 (March 1965), p. 28.

[9]Wilbur Cohen once characterized the range in opinions concerning the minimum floor as the difference between a rough pine floor and a warm Bigelow carpet. He noted that the term itself is a "facile" phrase that conceals the complexity of the issue. See Wilbur J. Cohen, "Federalism and Social Insurance," in *The American System of Social Insurance*, ed. Bowen, et al, p. 11.

For two opposing views on the proper balance between Social Security and private pensions see Bert Seidman, "Concepts of Balance between Social Security (OASDI) and Private Pension Benefits"; and Robert J. Myers, "Concepts of Balance between OASDI and Private Pension Benefits: A Partnership or, Instead, the Lion's Share for OASDI?" in *Social Security and Private Pension Plans: Competition or Complimentary?* ed., Dan M. McGill (Homewood, Ill.: Richard D. Irwin, 1977), chaps. 6 and 7.

because (1) it takes into account the size of the taxpayer's family, personal deductions, and total income (not just earnings); and (2) it is a progressive tax, thus imposing a relatively greater burden on the higher income groups. It is also a better automatic stabilizer.

By making up to half of the Social Security benefits taxable income for many beneficiaries (currently, about 10 percent of the total beneficiaries—but an increasing proportion in the future) and earmarking these taxes for the Social Security system, the 1983 amendments introduced some indirect general revenue financing. However, the only major use of nonearmarked general revenues has to been to pay well over half the cost of Supplementary Medical Insurance (in fact, somewhat over 75 percent currently). The other uses of nonearmarked general revenues were temporary measures designed to provide benefits to closed groups of beneficiaries. Except for SMI, the Social Security system is still in principle a self-supporting system.

Less than Full Funding

From the beginning, as noted earlier, Social Security has been less than fully funded. On the other hand, today the trust funds play a much smaller role than originally envisaged and less than had been the case up to 1972.

A major argument in favor of a larger trust fund is that the financial burden on future generations would be lessened. The cost of proposed benefit liberalizations would be more immediately apparent, and the rights of future benefit recipients would be more secure.

The major argument against a large trust fund is that, because the system is expected to operate indefinitely, all that is needed is a contingency fund. Furthermore, it is argued, a large trust fund may serve as an unwarranted excuse for increasing benefits or reducing eligibility requirements. Moreover, the higher taxes required to build a large trust fund would impose an undesirable burden on the economy. Finally, a trust fund makes a real contribution to the economic welfare of future generations only if it transfers funds from current consumption to investment, thus increasing productivity in the future. To increase productivity, instead of collecting more funds to build a large trust fund, it is more important to finance more adequately through taxes other public expenditures such as education and national defense and to encourage private investment.

A key assumption under less than full funding is that the system will continue to operate indefinitely, a subject to which we will return shortly.

A Contributory System

Social Security, except for SMI, is supported by both employee and employer contributions. Employees should contribute, it is argued, because (1) the problems of death, poor health, and old age are not entirely due to employment; (2) these contributions make possible higher benefits; (3) employees are made more aware of the cost of proposed liberalizations; (4) employee contributions strengthen the moral obligation of the government to provide benefits later; and (5) employees like the concept of receiving benefits they have earned through past contributions.

Employers have been asked to contribute for the same reasons that they have been encouraged to establish employee benefit plans plus the fact that Social Security reduces the cost of such private plans. Employers, it is said, also have a social obligation with respect to the entire system. For this last reason employer contributions, it is argued, should not be attributed to specific employees. At least part of the employer's contribution, it is argued, can be shifted to consumers and to employees.

Throughout its history the employee payroll tax has been a flat tax rate on the employee's earnings up to the maximum taxable earnings base. The employer pays a matching tax. Proposals that have been made but not enacted would have increased (1) the tax rates on present older workers to reduce the intergenerational transfers, (2) the payroll tax rate as the taxable earnings increase, and (3) the employer's share of the total taxes collected by applying the payroll tax rate to the employer's entire payroll amount.

Implied Intergenerational Contract

Implicit in the decision not to fund fully the Social Security system is an implied contract that the system will operate indefinitely and that future generations will pay out of their earnings some of the benefits to be received by the present generation. Many persons have questioned whether future generations of workers will honor this implied contract if they perceive that the income needs of the elderly are not as great as in the past and that they will not get their own money's worth from the system. What appears more likely, however, is that, at least for the foreseeable future, the basic compact will be honored, but the provisions will be altered because of the changing environment.

As Michael Taussig has noted, if the aged and their middle-aged allies had wanted to exploit the young, they could have exploited them much more than they have. The aged, however, do care about future generations who are, to many of the aged, their children and grandchildren. They do not want to impose undue burdens on future generations. Even if Social Security did not exist, transfers from the young to the old would still occur. Social Security permits the systematic social sharing of the total burden among both those who have retired or disabled persons to support and those who do not. Both the aged and the young can support such a system if the transfers are considered to be fair. Perceived fairness, therefore, is important if the system is to survive.[10]

Two recent views of the nature of this contract have been advanced by Richard Musgrave and John Fibiger. In Musgrave's opinion, because OASDI remains in a continuing state of disequilibrium, it "is important to clarify the nature of the social contract upon which the retirement system may be designed to rest and to consider its implications for the concept of system viability."[11] His solution is a contract under which the working population and retirees would share the risks created by uncertain future changes in productivity and population growth. Contributions and benefits would be adjusted each year (or every five years) to maintain a fixed ratio of the per capita earnings (net of contributions to OASDI) of workers to the per capita benefits paid to retirees.

---

[10]Colin D. Campbell, ed., *Financing Social Security* (Washington, D.C.: American Enterprise Institute for Public Policy Research, 1979), p. 222.

[11]Richard A. Musgrave, "A Reappraisal of Financing Social Security," in *Social Security Financing*, ed., Felicity Skidmore (Cambridge, Mass.: MIT Press, 1981), p. 96.

In commenting on Musgrave's paper, which he suspects would be difficult to implement, Fibiger described a two-stage social contract.[12] The first stage, currently in effect, is a general promise—a general memorandum of understanding—to new entrants to the labor force. When they retire, Social Security will still exist, though the benefits may be much different than at present. During the second stage this general memorandum will become a fairly strongly committed social contract. One possibility is a commitment among generations that the retirement age be adjusted to maintain a constant ratio of beneficiaries to workers.

The intergenerational contract may never become explicit, but an implicit contract remains a basic principle of Social Security.[13]

The Future? Revolution or Evolution

The future of Social Security will almost certainly include many major changes. These changes may be revolutionary or evolutionary.

Why Some Major Changes Are Likely

Two important reasons why these changes are likely are as follows. First, the system faces some serious financing problems. Second, highly significant social and cultural changes have made Social Security out-of-date in many respects.

Financial Problems. According to the 1985 Reports of the Boards of Trustees of the OASDHI Trust Funds, Social Security is in much better financial shape than it was a few short years ago.[14] A careful study of these reports, however, shows that the long-range forecast is not as reassuring as the short-range picture.

The Hospital Insurance Trust Fund is known to face both

---

[12]Skidmore, ed., *Social Security Financing*, pp. 169–70.

[13]Thomas Edwards has characterized this general understanding as an open-ended "IOU." See Campbell, ed., *Financing Social Security*, p. 309.

[14]Harry C. Ballantyne, "Actuarial Status of the OASI and DI Trust Funds," *Social Security Bulletin* 48, no. 6 (June 1985), pp. 27–31; Sol Mussey, "Actuarial Status of the HI and SMI Trust Funds," *Social Security Bulletin* 48, no. 6 (June 1985), pp. 32–40.

short-range and long-range problems. Under the intermediate B assumptions, during the 25-year period from 1985 through 2009, the annual costs expressed as a percentage of the corresponding taxable payrolls (including amounts for Trust Fund building and maintenance) are expected to average 3.57 percent. The annual contributions expressed as a percentage of the same payroll base are expected to average only 2.89 percent, resulting in an actuarial balance (average contribution rate minus average cost rate) of minus .68 percent. Under this set of assumptions, the HI Trust Fund will be exhausted in 1998.

In their 1984 Report the trustees estimated an actuarial balance for HI of minus 1.3 percent and exhaustion of the Trust Fund in 1991. Principally because of some reductions in the amounts paid medical providers for their services and the decreased rates of hospital utilization which have been experienced, the outlook is brighter today but still a cause for deep concern. An unusual feature of the 1985 report is that it also includes a 75-year actuarial balance calculation for HI. For the period 1985–2059, under the intermediate B assumptions, the costs are expected to average 5.69 percent of taxable payroll compared with a 2.90 percent average contribution rate, producing an actuarial balance of minus 2.79 percent. This 75-year estimate, of course, is subject to a wide margin of error, but it emphasizes how much the situation may worsen after the next 25 years. Faced with these short-run and long-run estimates, the Board recommended curtailments in the rate of growth of the HI program.

Supplementary Medical Insurance, according to the 1985 report, is financially sound in the sense that the premiums and general revenue appropriations through December 1985 are expected to be more than sufficient to cover projected benefit and administrative costs incurred through that date, including a reasonable allowance for projection error. The trustees, however, are deeply concerned about the rapid increase in the cost of the program over time and the increasing proportion of the costs that must be financed out of general revenues. For this reason they recommended curtailments in the rate of growth of SMI as well as HI.

OASDI is in much better financial shape, primarily because of the important 1983 amendments. The 1985 reports on the

OASI and DI Trust Funds state that, over the 1985–2059 period, under the intermediate B assumptions, costs will average 13.35 percent of taxable payrolls compared with a 12.94 income (mainly contributions) rate, causing an actuarial balance of minus .41 percent. Because the income rate is more than 95 percent of the cost rate, the system is considered to be in "close actuarial balance." During the next 25 years, the actuarial balance is a strong plus 2.00 percent, which will cause the combined trust funds to accumulate a substantial "surplus."

All, however, is not well in the long run with OASDI. The Reports indicate that, after the next 25 years, the average cost rates will exceed the average income rates by a substantial amount. During 2010–2034 the actuarial balance will be minus .78 percent and during 2035–2059, minus 2.46 percent. Eventually the expected large "surplus" of the OASDI Trust Funds will disappear.

An extremely important question is what will happen after the next 75 years. Each year the 75 years used for the long-range projections moves up one year. As surplus years are replaced by deficit years, a reasonable assumption in the short run, the actuarial deficit estimate will increase, other things being equal. Looking beyond the next 75 years is, of course, an extremely difficult assignment. It is difficult enough to estimate what will happen in 1986. However, not looking beyond the next 75 years may cause us to close our eyes to some impending problems. For example, in *The Actuarial Update,* Kenneth A. Steiner has calculated what the long-range actuarial balance will be at five-year intervals between 1985 and 2060, assuming that the intermediate assumptions and the relationship between income and outgo for the year 2060 continue indefinitely.[15] By 1990, the actuarial balance would fall from minus .41 percent to minus .62 percent. By 1992, the system would cease to be in "close actuarial balance." By 2010 the actuarial balance would be minus 1.85 percent, by 2035 (Social Security's 100th birthday year) it would be minus 2.38 percent, and by 2060 (when the fund balance would be exhausted), it would be minus 2.33 percent. Of

[15]Kenneth A. Steiner, "OASDI's Declining Actuarial Balance," *The Actuarial Update* 14, no. 9 (September 1985), pp. 4–5.

course, more optimistic or pessimistic assumptions after 2060 would produce a different outlook.[16] At some time, however, the system seems likely to require some adjustments to restore its close actuarial balance; one relatively simple one would be an increase in the combined employer-employee tax rate of about 2.4 percent, beginning in 2050. Fortunately, barring some economic conditions that are closer to the pessimistic assumptions used in the report, Congress will have time to plan these changes carefully.

Demographic, Economic, and Social Changes

Demographic, economic, and social changes affecting Social Security will not receive as much attention in this chapter as financing problems, but they are no less important. The American worker and the American family have changed greatly since the system was established in 1935.

In 1935, persons 65 or over were only about 6 percent of the population. Currently this proportion is about 13 percent and is expected to increase to about 12 to 13 percent by 2000 and 15 to 17 percent by 2020. Even more dramatic will be the increase in persons aged 85 and over. This increase in the proportion of the population who will be aged 65 or over is one reason for the higher average cost rates of Social Security after the turn of the century. The aged will also represent a higher percentage of the voters, and businesses and politicians will be more likely to cater to their needs. Life expectancies will also increase, causing more older working adults to have parents depending upon their emotional, if not financial, support. As their health improves, more of these aged persons may choose to work until more advanced ages. Their economic status should improve as more of them become eligible for private pensions and accumulate other savings prior to retirement.

In 1935, the stereotypical young American family was a husband who worked for pay, a wife who did not work for pay, and two or more children (but a significant proportion did not fit

[16]At the symposium at which this paper was presented, Robert J. Myers indicated that the actuarial deficits were overstated for those years in which the OASDI is expected to have a large surplus (because no account is taken of the interest earnings of the trust funds for a number of future years).

this mold). Only about 1.2 percent of the population 14 years and over was divorced; 32 percent were single. Because of the Great Depression, their standard of living was low.

By 1963, about 32 percent of the married couples included a wife in the labor force.[17] The number of children under 18 per family with children averaged about 2.4. The median family income was about $6,593. About 49 percent of the heads of households were high school graduates; 11 percent, college graduates. About 10 percent of these heads of households were women. Blue-collar workers still outnumbered white-collar workers, but the margin was decreasing. About 2.5 percent of the persons 14 and over were divorced; only 22 percent were single.

By 1983, over half of the married couples included a wife in the labor force. The number of children per family with children had dropped to about 1.9. The median family income had risen substantially to $27,450, increasing their purchasing power by 35 percent. The education of household heads had increased, with about 71 percent being high school graduates and 20 percent being college graduates. About 16 percent of these heads of households were women. White-collar workers outnumbered blue-collar workers by about 38 percent. About 7 percent of the persons 14 years or over were divorced, a sharp increase following domestic upheavals of the 1970s, when nearly one of every two marriages ended with divorce. Another result of these divorces and changes in lifestyles was that, by 1983, one of four households with children was headed by a single parent, and by 1990 the percent may reach as high as 50 percent. Single persons continued to represent 22 percent of the population.[18]

Married couples that include two wage earners, single-parent families that may soon match the number of married couples, more single persons among those aged 65 or under, fewer children, higher education levels, more purchasing power, and a much greater proportion of employees in the service industries, combined with more knowledge and experience with financial

---

[17] "The Average American Family, Then and Now," *U.S. News & World Report*, November 21, 1983, pp. 78–79.

[18] "Playing Both Mother and Father," *Newsweek*, July 15, 1985, p. 42.

planning, differentiate this and future generations of workers from their predecessors. Consequently they do and will have different Social Security needs and desires. Of course, some families will continue to include only one wage earner, some will have more than two children, many persons will not complete high school, others will be unemployed or employed at low wage levels, and many will not be financially sophisticated. Their needs and desires must also be recognized. The net effect of these changes will be a demand for changes in Social Security even if the financial problems noted earlier did not exist.

Proposed Revolutionary Changes

Several revolutionary changes have been proposed that would change the basic objectives and structure of Social Security. Some would change the name, as well as the program. Of the many proposals that have been made, three will be described here to illustrate the possibilities: (1) The Pechman, Aaron, Taussig Two-Tier System; (2) Ferrara's Ideal System; and (3) Robertson's Freedom Plan.[19]

---

[19]Some other proposals include the following:

1. Edgar K. Browning, "Social Insurance and Intergenerational Transfers," *Journal of Law and Economics* 16 (October 1973), pp. 215–37.
2. Michael J. Boskin, *The Crisis in Social Security: Problems and Prospects* (San Francisco: Institute for Contemporary Studies, 1977), chap. 8.
3. James M. Buchanan, "Social Insurance in a Growing Economy: A Proposal for Radical Reform," *National Tax Journal* (December, 1968), pp. 386–95.
4. Martin Feldstein, "Toward a Reform of Social Security," *Public Interest*, Summer 1975, pp. 75–95.
5. Milton J. Friedman, "Second Lecture" in *Social Security: Universal or Selective?* ed. Wilbur J. Cohen and Milton Friedman (Washington, D.C.: American Enterprise Institute, 1972), pp. 21–49.
6. Charles D. Hobbs and Stephen Powlesland, *Retirement Security Reform: Restructuring the Social Security System* (Concord, Vt: Institute for Liberty and Community, 1975).
7. Arthur B. Laffer and R. David Ranson, "A Proposal for Reforming Social Security," in *Income Support Policies for the Aged*, ed., George S. Tolley and Richard Burkhauser (Cambridge, Mass.: Ballinger, 1977).
8. Carolyn L. Weaver, *Understanding the Sources and Dimensions of Crisis in Social Security: A First Step toward Meaningful Reform* (Arlington, Va: Fiscal Policy Council, 1981).

For an excellent, short description of these proposals and other Social Security issues see Lawrence H. Thompson, "The Social Security Reform Debate," *Journal of Economic Literature* 21 (December 1983), pp. 1425–67.

Pechman-Aaron-Taussig Two-Tier System. Perhaps the first revolutionary proposal to attract widespread attention was made by Pechman, Aaron, and Taussig in their 1968 book entitled *Social Security: Perspectives for Reform.* They suggested that OASDI be divided into two systems because the current system attempts "to solve two problems with one instrument—how to prevent destitution among the aged poor and how to assure to people, having adequate incomes before retirement, benefits that are related to their previous standard of living."[20] The two replacement systems would include (1) a negative income tax program that would provide at least a minimum subsistence standard of living for families of all sizes, and (2) a system that would replace the same proportion (say, one half) of lost income at all earnings levels between a subsistence level and the median earnings level. Above the median earnings level the replacement rate would decrease. No dependents' benefits would be paid under this system. Each beneficiary would claim the better of the two benefits. Both systems would be financed through income taxes.

The social adequacy objective would be separated from the private equity objective. The authors favored this approach because they believed it would be more efficient and more flexible. Either system could be altered without affecting the other, except at the margin. The cost of achieving each of the two objectives would be identifiable. They justified government participation in a strictly wage-related program because of (1) shortcomings in individual savings decisions with respect to retirement needs, investment selection, and inflation; (2) the inadequacies of private pensions; and (3) the cost to other members of society if a person does not prepare adequately for retirement.

Although the authors recommended this two-tier system as a long-term goal, they recognized that it would be very expensive and highly controversial. In 1980, in a thoughtful review of a paper on two-tier systems, one of the authors, Henry Aaron, acknowledged that he had changed his mind about the desirability of such an approach. He noted that he could not point to

---

[20]Joseph A. Pechman, Henry J. Aaron, and Michael K. Taussig, *Social Security Perspectives for Reform* (Washington, D.C.: The Brookings Institution, 1968), p. 215.

any analytical advance to explain his switch, just a revision of political prejudice. In addition, he stated that "major structural reforms are easier to enact when present law can be liberalized than when it cannot. The budgetary limits so very much with us today suggest that the best prospect for improving the equity with which social security treats the diversity of modern families is through modifications in the present program structure."[21]

In *The Future of Social Security,* Alicia Munnell suggested a modified version of this two-tier proposal.[22] Instead of a negative income tax she favored an expanded means-tested Supplemental Security Income program. Instead of a wage-related system that reduced the replacement rate for higher than median earnings she would provide equal replacement rates above all earnings levels. SSI would be supported by general revenues, the wage-related system by payroll taxes. She argued that (1) shifting the welfare burden to SSI would rationally distribute the total burden of income maintenance, (2) a proportional wage-related benefit structure would guarantee all future workers an equitable return on their contributions, (3) workers would be more likely to regard their payroll taxes as savings, and (4) workers might be permitted to opt out of the strictly wage system provided they could demonstrate they had made equivalent arrangements elsewhere.

A third closely related proposal is a "double-decker" system. The principal difference between this system and the two-tier systems described above is that the first tier would be a demogrant payable to each aged person, disabled person, or surviving child. The 1979 Advisory Council on Social Security rejected a double-decker proposal that would have paid (1) a flat demogrant of about $122 a month plus (2) 30 percent of the worker's Average Indexed Monthly Earnings (AIME) to persons with covered earnings records.[23] Opponents argued that such a

---

[21]Henry Aaron, Discussion of the Munnell-Stiglin paper, in *A Challenge to Social Security: The Changing Roles of Women and Men in American Society*, ed. Richard V. Burkhauser and Karen C. Holder (New York: Academic Press, 1982), p. 127.

[22]Alicia H. Munnell, *The Future of Social Security* (Washington, D.C.: The Brookings Institution, 1977), pp. 38–44.

[23]*Reports of the 1979 Advisory Council on Social Security*, chap. 4.

radical change would alter the benefit structure in ways they considered undesirable and would create some important risks. For example, they noted that benefits would be reduced for many dependents and survivors, the demogrant would be expensive, people would receive the demogrant regardless of need, and the demogrant, which might be frozen at $122, would not do enough for the truly needy. On the other hand, as compared with the two-tier system, the absence of a means test would reduce the cost of administration and the stigma, if any, associated with such a test.[24]

Ferrara's Ideal System. In *Social Security: The Inherent Contradiction,* Peter J. Ferrara described an ideal system that would be much more revolutionary than either the two-tier or double-decker programs. The strength of his feeling about this program is indicated by the following quote:

> The benefits of this long-term reform are remarkable to contemplate. All the problems we discussed in earlier chapters will be solved and there will be several additional benefits as well. Everyone in society will benefit from this proposal and no one will be made worse off. Consequently all should support it.[25]

Ferrara summarized the most serious shortcomings of the present programs as follows:

> The most sophisticated econometric studies show that the program is needlessly costing Americans hundreds of billions of dollars annually because of its negative impacts on the economy. Other studies show that young people entering the sytem today will never receive a fair return on all the social security taxes they will pay into the program over the course of their lives. The program is fundamentally coercive, forcing all Americans to participate regardless of their desires. It imposes on all Americans a single insurance plan with a particular set of provisions instead of allowing a system of diverse options that would permit individuals and their families to choose a specific plan suited to their needs.

---

[24]In 1980 Alicia Munnell and Laura Stiglin compared how women would fare under the present system, a two-tier earnings sharing plan, and a double-decker plan. See Alicia H. Munnell and Laura E. Stiglin, "Women and the Two-Tier Social Security System," in *A Challenge to Social Security*, ed. Burkhauser and Holder, chap. 5.

[25]Peter J. Ferrara, *Social Security: The Inherent Contradiction* (San Francisco: Cato Institute, 1980), p. 391. The reform is explained on pp. 370–91. For a more recent version see Peter J. Ferrara, *Social Security: Avoiding the Crisis* (Washington, D.C.: Cato Institute, 1982), pp. 101–33.

> The inequities and negative economic impacts of the system fall most heavily on some of the most vulnerable groups in society—blacks, the poor, women, the elderly, and the young. The program is financed by a regressive payroll tax that causes economic inefficiency and imposes a hardship on the poor. Despite recent tax increases and official assurances, the danger that the system will become bankrupt remains real.[26]

Not all persons, of course, would agree with this assessment, but Ferrara's arguments and proposals merit serious study. After examining the major reform proposals made prior to 1980, he proposed an Ideal System that would be preceded by short-term reforms. Only the long-term reform will be described here.

First, the welfare elements in the present Social Security system would be transferred to SSI. Second, the remaining Social Security system would be transformed as follows:

1. Invite private institutions to apply for listing their finished products among the investment alternatives to the transformed Social Security. These products would be packages of retirement, survivor, disability, and perhaps hospital insurance. The government would guarantee approved investments.
2. Calculate the age below which individuals could receive more in retirement benefits from these private plans than from the present Social Security program. He estimates this age to be 40. This estimate assumes that the employee could invest in the private plans with both the employer and the employee making contributions and that the real rate of return on the private investments would be more than 3 percent.
3. Require persons below age 40 to save a certain percentage of their incomes for retirement and insurance protection. This percentage would not exceed the current combined employer-employee payroll tax rate. These savings could be used to purchase one of the approved private alternatives, in which case these persons would receive no Social Security benefits for their past contributions, or they could stay in the transformed Social Security program. If they elect to

[26]Ferrara, *Social Security: The Inherent Contradiction*, pp. 3–4.

stay under Social Security, their benefits will equal all their past and future contributions increased by the rate of inflation, not the presently prescribed benefits.

4. Give persons between age 40 and 60 Social Security bonds that mature upon retirement. At maturity the bonds would purchase the benefits currently promised under Social Security minus the amount they could earn if they invested their future payroll taxes in one of the private alternatives. Alternatively they could invest these moneys in Social Security bonds indexed for inflation that would be expected to yield less than the private alternatives.
5. Continue the present Social Security benefits for persons over age 60. These benefits and the Social Security bonds granted immediately to persons between age 40 and 60 would be financed by general revenues.
6. Expand the tax incentives so that individuals will receive tax free the full value of the increased production created by the investments they make in the private alternatives.

Robertson's Freedom Plan. The final proposal to be discussed is noteworthy because it was advanced by A. Haeworth Robertson, who was chief actuary of the Social Security Administration from 1975 to 1978. In *The Coming Revolution in Social Security,* Haeworth presents a highly readable description of the system that he helped to administer but believes should be replaced by a Freedom Plan.[27] This plan is based on the premise that an individual can anticipate old age and should make financial plans, including the purchase of insurance, accordingly. Government should be involved in this planning only because of (1) inflation, (2) unpredictable abnormally long life spans, and (3) misfortunes, financial or health related, not reasonably controllable by the individual in financial planning. Similarly, except for the reasons just specified, an individual should be able to plan for the needs of his or her family in case he or she should be injured, contract a sickness, or die prematurely.

According to Robertson, a completely new type of Social

---

[27] A. Haeworth Robertson, *The Coming Revolution in Social Security* (McLean, Va.: Security Press, 1981), chaps. 27–29.

Security system for the younger segment of the population deserves serious consideration because the present system is complex; trespasses on our personal lives by affecting such decisions as when to retire, when to divorce, and when to remarry; divides the population into two groups—those who work and those who are inactive but share in the goods and services produced; discourages personal savings; rewards life patterns that are becoming less representative of modern life; and hides any connection between an individual's benefits and taxes.

On a specified date (Robertson originally suggested July 4, 1984), for all persons under age 45 Robertson would replace Social Security with a Freedom Plan. Older persons would still be covered under OASDHI. The Freedom Plan would have the following components:

1. A mandatory Senior Citizen Benefit program, financed by general revenues, that would provide each eligible person at age 70 a tax-free minimum level of support. The only eligibility requirement would be resident citizenship for at least 25 years since age 35. Each year the benefit level would be increased to match some cost-of-living index.
2. Freedom Bonds sold by the government that would pay no interest but would be indexed to maintain their purchasing power. Individuals between ages 45 and 70 could invest up to 10 percent of their earnings in these bonds. At retirement age they could exchange their bonds for an indexed pension. If the worker died prior to retirement, survivors could claim the face value of the Freedom Bonds.
3. Cost-of-living supplements provided by the government for those workers receiving private pensions.
4. A monthly cash benefit equal to the Senior Citizen Benefit for persons totally disabled for 12 full months who met minimum labor force attachments and residency requirements and who agree to participate in a qualified rehabilitation and retraining program.
5. Medical care benefits closely resembling current Medicare benefits for all citizens aged 70 and over who had been residents for at least 25 years since they were age 35. Persons receiving monthly disability cash benefits would also

qualify for these medical benefits.

6. All benefits under the Freedom Plan would be financed on a current cost basis through general revenues. The tax used to generate these revenues would be clearly identified as a Freedom Plan Tax.
7. A supplementary welfare plan, financed by general revenues, would provide death, disability, and medical expense benefits for the needy.

Why These Differences from the Traditional Model? Lawrence Thompson attributes differences in opinion about the need for or desirable direction for Social Security reform to which of three conceptual models the analyst prefers.[28] The models differ, he states, in (1) whether they focus on current-year transfers or transfers over the life cycle (consumption reduced during working years and increased during retirement), and (2) whether they view certain differences in benefits as evidence of redistribution or as the ex post result of an ex ante insurance arrangement. The three models are (1) the tax transfer model (illustrated by the Pechman, Aaron, and Taussig Two-Tier system), (2) the insurance or traditional model, and (3) the annuity-welfare model (illustrated by Ferrara's Ideal Plan). The first focuses exclusively on current-year transfers; the second emphasizes the life-cycle approach; and the third treats the welfare component as a current-year transfer and the annuity component as a life-cycle transfer. "Subscribing to one or another of the models conditions one particular analyst to see a serious problem where another sees a perfectly rational arrangement."[29]

As Thompson has observed, the present system emphasizes (1) financial viability and predictability in the long run, and (2) income support that preserves the beneficiaries' dignity and self-respect. Other objectives, such as avoiding adverse effects on savings and the supply of labor, have received less attention. Analysts disagree on the effects of various reforms on these

---

[28]Thompson, "Social Security Reform Debate," pp. 1436–38.

[29]Ibid., p. 1438.

other objectives.[30] Additional research is required, but choosing among the many possible objectives requires "social value judgments that can only be resolved in the political arena."[31]

Proposed Evolutionary Changes

The boundary line between proposed revolutionary and evolutionary changes is fuzzy, but in this chapter a proposed change will be considered evolutionary if it would not change either the benefit or financing structure in basic ways. The changes might be considered "tinkering" with the system, but the effects might be major, not minor.

Some evolutionary changes that have been advocated frequently or strongly enough to be reasonable candidates for evolutionary changes in the benefit or financing structure are summarized briefly below. Most of these change are designed to reduce benefit costs or to adjust the system for changes in the work force and the American family. The list is not meant to be exhaustive.

1. Raise the normal retirement age above the current scheduled age 67 to either age 68 or 70.
2. Increase immediately the percentage increase for delaying retirement beyond the normal retirement age from the present 3 percent a year to the 8 percent scheduled to become effective on a gradual basis during 1990 to 2009.[32]
3. Use a price index to calculate the average indexed monthly earnings instead of an earnings index unless the earnings index increase is less.
4. Change the primary insurance amount formula so that the PIA continues to decrease as a percentage of the AIME as the AIME increases, but not as rapidly. This recommendation is consistent with what appears to be a trend toward

---

[30]For an excellent summary of the many but inconclusive studies on how Social Security has affected savings and the supply of labor, see George F. Break, "The Economic Effects of the OASI Program," and the comments by Henry Aaron and Robert Reischauer in Skidmore, ed., *Social Security Financing*, pp. 45–88.

[31]Thompson, "Social Security Reform Debate," p. 1463.

[32]For an important paper on this change see Robert J. Myers, "Income of Social Security Beneficiaries as Affected by Earnings Test and Income Taxes on Benefits," *The Journal of Risk and Insurance* no. 2 (June 1985), pp. 289–300.

more emphasis on private equity. Trends change, however, and some persons favor changing the formula in the opposite direction.

5. Introduce some form of earnings sharing for married couples into the determination of the cash benefits or provide a working-spouse benefit (so that some recognition is given to the higher contributions of a two-worker family).[33]
6. Eliminate the earnings test for persons who have reached or passed the normal retirement age or accelerate the $1 for $3 reduction that is scheduled to become effective in 1990.
7. Index the cash benefits for less than the increase in the consumer price index and never more than the increase in average national earnings.
8. Eliminate the cash benefits for dependents of retired or disabled workers. Alternative suggestions would reduce these benefits by lowering the current percentages by, say, one third or by substituting dollar amounts that are the same for all PIAs.[34]
9. Eliminate the $255 lump-sum death benefit. Some persons, however, favor increasing this benefit to, say, $1,000.
10. Liberalize slightly the statutory definition of disability so that for older workers the test is inability to perform their own occupation.
11. Set the Medicare eligibility age equal to the OASDI normal retirement age.
12. Change the Medicare benefits so that they provide slightly less protection for short-term illnesses and more protection for long-term illnesses.
13. Continue to index the maximum taxable earnings base for employees, but have employers pay taxes based on their entire payroll.

---

[33]For an excellent discussion of earnings sharing and related proposals such as homemakers' credits and child-care drop-out years, see Burkhauser and Holden, eds., *A Challenge to Social Security,* chap. 5.

[34]An alternative approach would impose higher tax rates on workers who would expect to have dependents. See Laurence J. Kotlikoff, "Reforming Social Security for the Young: A Framework for Consensus," in *Controlling the Cost of Social Security* ed., Colin D. Campbell (Washington, D.C.: American Enterprise Institute of Public Policy Research, 1984), pp. 93–94.

14. Continue to support the system mainly on payroll taxes, but increase the role of general revenues. One common recommendation is to finance Hospital Insurance partially or completely with general revenues. Another proposal would in addition fund part of the cash benefits with general revenues. The objective would be to fund in this way all or part of the dependents' benefits, the minimum benefits, and possibly the intergenerational benefit transfers. This general revenue contribution, however, should not exceed one third of the total and be derived from earmarked income taxes.

What Will Happen?

Forecasting what will actually happen to the Social Security system is a hazardous assignment. As a weather forecaster during World War II, I experienced the difficulty of predicting how nature will behave in the short run. Predicting how people will change the Social Security system in, say, the next 25 years is much more difficult.

My best guess, however, is that the changes will be evolutionary, not revolutionary. I share the previously expressed view of Henry Aaron that in a time of tight budgets, which I expect to continue, major structural reforms are difficult to enact.

Among the proposals listed among the evolutionary changes, the ones I believe have the highest chance of being accepted are (1) an increase in the scheduled normal retirement age to 68; (2) an accelerated increase in the delayed retirement credit to 8 percent a year; (3) some form of earnings sharing for married couples; (4) some reduction in dependents' benefits, especially for higher paid workers; (5) continued reliance mainly on payroll taxes, but an increased use of general revenues, probably in Hospital Insurance; and (6) possibly indexing cash benefits for less than the increase in the CPI. What one can more safely predict, however, is that the debate will feature many proposals that have not yet been conceived and that some major changes not foreseeable at present will occur.

Future Policies for Employer-Based Pension Plans

6

by William F. May*

The purpose of this chapter is to present a businessman's perspective on improving the long-run contribution of employer-based pension plans in providing retirement income. While my recommendations for future policy changes are my own, I have been strongly influenced by the work of my fellow trustees at the Committee for Economic Development (CED).

Within the past few years I have participated, with a group of CED business leaders and academic advisers, in the preparation of two important CED publications—*Reforming Retirement Policies* (1981) and *Social Security: From Crisis to Crisis?* (1984). We believe these CED statements, representing the joint efforts of such business leaders as Bill Greenough of TIAA–CREF and Bob Beck of Prudential, and academicians such as Dan McGill, influenced the legislation which liberalized the concept of IRAs and the 1983 amendments to restore the solvency of the Social Security system. Our approach to reforming retirement policies recognizes the importance of strengthening employer-based pension plans as part of an overall strategy which includes increased individual saving and a strengthened Social Security

*Chairman, Research and Policy Committee, Committee for Economic Development.

system for meeting the basic income needs of elderly Americans.

Since CED's recent work on reforming retirement policy, other organizations and individual researchers have continued to generate the type of analyses so essential to the development of policies for increasing the role of employer pensions as a source of retirement income. At CED we have benefited significantly from the excellent research recently completed by the Employee Benefits Research Institute.[1] Some of the ideas I wish to present are based partially on Dr. Andrews' publication and the work of other researchers.

There are three main components in the development of a strategy to increase the contribution of employer-based plans to retirement income in the next century. First, we must recognize the growing importance this source of retirement income has already played, and will continue to play, in improving the economic security for workers in the middle and upper ends of the wage spectrum. Second, it is critical that we set priorities among pension issues and assess their significance in relation to the purpose of employer-based plans for retirement income in the next century. Some of these issues are important; in my opinion, others are relatively insignificant and the continuing debate over their importance is simply distracting our attention from achieving the truly important long-run goal of employer-based pension plans.

Finally, management, labor, and public officials should concentrate their attention on what policies we need to introduce now, so that future elderly generations will receive an increasing share of their retirement income from employer-based plans.

The Success of Employer-Based Pension Plans

The good news about employer plans is that they are now contributing to the retirement income of an increasing proportion

[1]See the excellent analyses of pension issues by Emily S. Andrews, *The Changing Profile of Pensions in America* (Washington, D.C.: Employee Benefit Research Institute, 1985).

of the elderly. Since 1970, contributions to employer-based plans have been increasing at a rate of about 12 percent per year. In 1971, 8 percent of elderly married couples received pensions from public employers and, by 1982, 15 percent were recipients of public pensions. Over the same period the recipiency rate for private-sector pensions increased from 23 percent to 33 percent.[2]

Since the early 1970s, benefit payments have been increasing at about 17 percent per year. For married couples over 65 years of age the median annual pension income from public plans increased about two and a half times to $7,320 in 1982, and for private-sector plans the income from this source doubled to $3,160. Unfortunately, double-digit rates of inflation in the latter part of the 1970s sharply curtailed the real value of pension benefits, which reached a plateau in 1978.

As the pension system matures, more and more of the elderly will receive part of their retirement income from employer plans. Over the past two decades the rate of pension participation among private-sector nonagricultural workers over 25 years of age rose from about 53 percent in 1960 to about 76 percent in 1975. The vesting rate has increased even more rapidly, and by 1980 over 45 percent of this group were vested in a private sector plan.[3] This growth in participation and vesting rates means that by the next century well over half of all elderly couples will be receiving income from employer plans.

The extension of pension coverage and improvements in pension benefits is part of the reason why, on an after-tax basis, the average income of the elderly is now about the same as that of the rest of the population.[4] Policies to stimulate the growth of pension plans are now providing most workers with an extremely efficient means of saving during their working lives so that they can consume part of their lifetime earnings during retirement.

Another advantage of the growth of pensions is that their as-

---

[2]Ibid., chap. 6.

[3]*Reforming Retirement Policies* (New York: Committee for Economic Development, 1981), p. 19.

[4]*Strategy for U.S. Industrial Competitiveness* (New York: Committee for Economic Development, 1984); *1985 Economic Report of the President* (Washington, D.C.: U. S. Government Printing Office, 1985), chap. 5.

sets are now an enormously important source of funds for capital investment throughout all sectors of the economy. In 1983 private pension plans held an estimated $1 trillion in assets and public plans held almost $300 billion. This represents a tenfold increase since 1950.[5] Our system of employer-based pensions provides an important vehicle to encourage individual saving. This is especially significant since we must raise the rate of capital investment if we are to match the productivity growth rates of our international competitors.[6]

The significant tax advantages to saving through employer-based pensions have produced a substantial increase in saving and investment. Empirical estimates suggest that about one half of the increase in pension fund assets represent a net addition to saving.[7] More generous Social Security benefits through the transfer of wealth from future generations of workers to present and future retirees cannot demonstrate a similar growth in saving for the capital investment necessary to improve the nations's future productivity growth. Both labor and business have good reason to be pleased that this growth of pension plans has moved closer to the original retirement income goals envisaged in the 1950s. Pension plans are now increasing the economic security of a larger share of the labor force and contributing to the long-run performance of the economy.

Modifying Current Pension Regulations

Much of the current debate over pension policy is concerned with proposed changes in pension regulations. In some cases the proponents of reform feel that current regulations are inequitable or that the regulations unnecessarily reduce the economic return from the investment of pension fund assets.

Several of the current criticisms of ERISA regulations have been persistent but unconvincing. I would place the following issues in this category:

---

[5]Richard Ippolito, *Pensions, Economics and Public Policy* (Homewood, Ill.: Richard D. Irwin, a Pension Research Council Monograph 1986), chap. 1.

[6]*Productivity Policy: Key to the Nation's Economic Future* (New York: Committee for Economic Development, 1983).

[7]Richard Ippolito, *Pensions, Economics and Public Policy*, chap. 9.

1. *The need to change the prohibited transactions provisions for investing pension fund assets.* Some critics believe that current fiduciary regulations should be changed to permit fund trustees and managers to use the assets to pursue social goals. Obviously some small part of pension fund portfolios could be invested to finance worthy causes or avoid support of unworthy ones without seriously reducing the rate of return. But any significant attempt to pursue social investing goals will inevitably reduce the rate of return and harm the plan participants. Modification of the prohibited transactions provisions for this purpose is not desirable.

2. *Require employers to contribute to the pension fund of employees who continue to work past age 65.* The justification for this proposal is based on the need to coordinate ERISA regulations with the Age Discrimination in Employment Act. I have a vested interest in this specific reform since I have reached retirement age, having worked in both private industry and in an academic position, and I am currently working toward a third career. Nevertheless, I believe the importance of this hotly debated issue is highly exaggerated.

Only about 12 percent of those over 65 years old are active in the labor force and most are in relatively high-paying jobs. By custom, and in law, seniority is a permissible criterion in setting wage rates. While some workers must continue to work beyond 65 years of age, I suspect that some workers' salaries are greater than their contributions to their firm's output. Employers may justify high salaries for these long-service employees because the overall cost of employing them is reduced by eliminating the employer contribution to these workers' pensions. If employers were required to contribute to the pensions of these workers it might discourage employment for those past 65 years of age.

3. *Employee rights when an employer terminates a pension plan and establishes a new defined-benefit or a new defined-contribution plan.* The issue concerns only the termination of defined-benefit plans which are fully funded. Under current law an employer may terminate a fully funded defined-benefit plan and start a new plan so long as it has fully vested all participants' benefits and has purchased and distributed annuity contracts in the appropriate amount. Any surplus assets may then revert to the employer.

Critics claim that the employees should share in this surplus. Unlike a defined-contribution plan, a defined-benefit plan is simply a promise to pay a retiree a future retirement income based on a formula established under the plan. I do not believe employees have a claim to any surplus assets on plan termination. Nevertheless, determining when a pension plan is fully funded and the magnitude of surplus assets is difficult since the funding status of a plan depends on the accuracy of long-range projections. Since improvements in the funding status of pension plans has benefited greatly from the rise in the value of assets over a relatively short period of time, we have to be cautious about assuming that the valuation of assets will continue to remain in surplus well into the future. Reversion of assets on termination of fully funded plans is a legitimate management goal, but I would suggest it only prudent of management to retain some of the surplus asset value in reserve when a new defined-benefit plan is established to offset any future unexplained decline in asset values.

The major issue concerning this type of plan termination is whether the employer should be able to benefit from the tax-sheltered investment income on the excess assets. On termination, I believe these excess interest earnings should revert to the U.S. Treasury.

While this is not a high priority for pension reform, it seems unfortunate that there is no way to permit the employer to have immediate access to the surplus assets without having to incur the cost of terminating the existing plan. If this were possible it would also avoid the natural anxiety which employees feel when the plan is terminated even though their right to a future pension is secure. From the point of view of employees it is also important to avoid terminating a plan since the fear of insufficient retirement income is one of the greatest sources of insecurity among older employees.

Pension Reform Priorities for the 21st Century

Many of the proposals to modify ERISA regulations are worthy of consideration and should be debated. I do, however, urge representatives of business and labor, as well as pension experts, to focus on the reforms we need now if employer-based pensions are to meet the retirement goals of current and future generations of workers and contribute to the long-run performance of the economy in the next century. It is a serious mistake to devote all our efforts to minor changes in regulations without considering the important reforms necessary to meet the long-run goals of pension policy.

If employer-based pensions are to be a more important component of our national retirement policy, we must consider future demographic and economic trends. The demographic characteristics of the population during the early part of the next century will be dominated by the retirement of the baby-boom generation. There is a great deal of controversy over the extent to which Social Security should provide retirement income for this group of retirees. Our present policy, as developed in the 1983 Social Security reforms, is to gradually raise trust fund revenues by increasing the taxes paid by employers and employees and raise the age at which Social Security benefits are paid early in the next century. It is hoped that the buildup in the trust fund during the 1990s will be sufficient to pay Social Security benefits to the Baby Boomers after about 2020.

The success of this strategy will depend on three factors: the growth of the working-age population, future productivity growth, and the willingness of the working population to accept a declining, and for some groups a negative, rate of return from their payment of Social Security taxes. At the Committee for Economic Development, we believe this strategy is not only inequitable but is likely to fail. We predict that the Social Security trust fund will again be threatened with insolvency about 2020. In addition, as young workers realize that their rate of return from Social Security will be significantly lower than the return to the retirees whose benefits they are paying, support for the system will decline.[8]

As labor, business, and policymakers attempt to develop a national pension policy, I believe that we must gradually

---

[8]*Social Security: From Crisis to Crisis?* (New York: Committee for Economic Development, 1984).

reduce reliance on Social Security as a source of retirement income and increase the importance of employer-based pensions and individual saving. To achieve this goal business must be prepared to support policies which will increase pension coverage and increase the proportion of the work force eligible for future pension benefits.

Increasing Pension Benefit Entitlement

The growth of employer-sponsored plans over the past two decades has led many to assume that another 20 years of this trend is inevitable and that by the beginning of the next century almost all workers over 21 years of age will have an opportunity to participate in employer-based pension plans throughout most of their work-force experience. The continued growth rate of these plans is, however, uncertain. Since 1979 the number of workers covered by employer-based plans has declined. Is this a temporary phenomenon brought about by the loss of employment in industries with well-developed plans (e.g., steel and textiles), or has pension coverage reached a plateau?

In my opinion, the number of workers covered by a pension will again increase as the economy expands, but it is uncertain whether the proportion of the work force with pension coverage will increase. There are currently some notable coverage gaps among some groups of workers. For example, among workers in firms with fewer than 100 workers only 37 percent can expect a future benefit entitlement, and if the firm is not unionized the proportion with an entitlement declines to 28 percent.[9] Lack of pension coverage is also more prevalent among young workers, workers with few years on the job, and those with low earnings. Over time the entitlement rate will rise as workers get older, remain on the job long enough to be eligible for a vested pension, and earn higher wages which come with seniority, but workers in smaller firms are unlikely to have sufficient access to employer-based pensions.

For workers who have relatively low earnings throughout their careers, Social Security should continue to be the predom-

---

[9]Emily S. Andrews, *Changing Profile*, chap. 3.

inant source of retirement income. If the business community believes, as I do, that there are significant economic advantages in strengthening the role of employer-based pensions as a source of retirement income, business must be prepared to support policies which will increase the rate of entitlement to pension benefits and extend coverage to those groups of workers who have poor access to employer plans.

Increasing Pension Benefit Entitlement

For almost 15 years there has been a constant debate over whether or not to liberalize the vesting requirements under ERISA. Many have proposed that the three alternative vesting standards under ERISA be modified to require that employees be vested after five years of participation in a pension. Adoption of a 5-year vesting standard rather than the 10-year alternative typically used in employer-based plans, would immediately add over a million men and about three quarters of a million women to the ranks of vested workers. It would benefit the 15 percent of workers who worked only five to nine years with their current employer just prior to retirement. According to one study, in 1979 the average family pension benefits of persons aged 40 to 44 would be expected to rise by about 9 percent under 5-year vesting compared to 10-year vesting.[10]

Within both the labor and business communities there is some resistance to moving to five-year vesting. Adoption of a five-year vesting standard will initially increase employee benefit costs, perhaps raising the cost of pension plan contributions by several percentage points of total contribution costs. Workers themselves will eventually bear some of the cost of earlier vesting in the form of lower wage increases or offsetting reductions in other features of their benefit package. In some cases it may even deter employers from starting new plans for their employees.

These trade-offs for earlier vesting pose problems, but I do not think they are insurmountable. I suggest we can avoid the immediate adverse effect of earlier vesting by phasing in the change over five or more years. This should provide employers

[10]Ibid., chap. 8.

and employees with the opportunity to restructure their entire compensation system and work out the type of benefit arrangements most suitable to the economic position of their firm.

Extension of Coverage

Earlier vesting will increase coverage of workers, especially among women and younger workers who have a tendency to change jobs frequently. On the other hand, earlier vesting is unlikely to reach the employees who do not now have pension coverage, many of whom work for small firms. It is estimated that if firms with less than 100 employees had the same coverage rate as firms with 100 to 500 employees, about 7.5 million additional workers would be enrolled in employer-based pension plans.

Proposals to extend coverage to all segments of the work force have ranged from mandatory minimum pension plans as proposed in the 1981 *Report of the President's Commission on Pension Policy* to more recent proposals which would permit small employers to make contributions to large pension funds managed by insurance companies and banks. Mandating pension plan coverage is likely to retard employment growth, especially among small employers. Permitting small employers to participate in larger plans may reduce some of the administrative costs associated with establishing and maintaining a pension plan and represents a more promising approach. It is doubtful, however, whether this is a sufficiently strong incentive for employers to establish a plan.

Based on my experience in business I am convinced that one of the most important employee concerns is that they will have sufficient income on retirement. The fact that pension plan coverage is strongly correlated with unionization suggests that if employees have an opportunity to express their own views they are likely to prefer some form of pension plan and to trade off wages for this benefit. I believe there are many advantages, both for the firm and for the workers, if employees are given some options among the components of the total compensation package. Perhaps the most appropriate way to extend pension coverage is to give employees the choice of whether or not they wish their employer to establish a pension plan.

One of the advantages of writing this chapter is that I can suggest new ideas with the caveat that the pension experts have to work out the details. Let me suggest a possible approach to extending coverage. Suppose all employers who do not have an employer-based pension plan were required to establish a 401(k) plan for their employees and provide payroll deductions for contributions to the plan *if* a majority of the employees voted for establishing a plan. The contributions would be voluntary, and employees would be given options on how to distribute their overall compensation among wages and fringe benefits. The employer would incur some administrative costs, but competition among benefit consultants and benefit fund managers would ensure that these costs would be minimized. It might even be worth considering giving small employers a one-time tax credit to offset the initial cost of establishing the plan.

I am sure there are many difficulties inherent in my proposal, but I believe pension experts should attempt to resolve them. I am also convinced that if business continues to argue for a greater role for employment-based pensions in the retirement income of future generations it has a responsibility to support innovative approaches to extending pension coverage.

There are also important economic trends which make it essential to initiate reforms in current pension policy. The occupational/industrial structure of the U.S. economy in the 21st century will be vastly different from what it is today. Economic change is a continuous process, and pension policy, as well as the bargaining decisions of labor and management, must not impede the ability of the labor force to adapt to change. The inevitability of structural change makes it essential to reassess current pension policy. In my opinion, a number of key issues need to be addressed to improve the future of employer-based pensions.

Negotiated Improvements in Pension Benefits Must Be Related to Overall Compensation and Future Productivity Growth

Over the past two decades management and labor have frequently negotiated pension benefits on the assumption that demand for the firm's output and its productivity performance were in a constant growth pattern. In manufacturing we often made pension benefit improvements retroactive so that workers close to retirement as well as retirees would share in the improved benefits. Everyone was guaranteed improved benefits out of expected future productivity growth. Unfortunately, in most industries, productivity growth came to a virtual halt by the end of the 1970s, and many of our industries with the most generous employment-based pensions experience severe competition from foreign and domestic competitors with relatively high levels of productivity.

Adjustment to the new competitive environment was a painful experience for both management and labor in many manufacturing industries. Because of the high cost of providing retroactive pension benefits, the adjustment process frequently took the form of unemployment for low-seniority workers. In the future we can avoid some of these problems if compensation, including pension benefits, is linked to *actual* productivity improvements. Workers should be entitled to share in the firm's productivity growth during their working careers—that is a primary reason why initial pension benefits are linked to the worker's earnings during the last few years prior to retirement. But we cannot guarantee increased pension benefits in the belief that high rates of future productivity growth are inevitable. To do so will ultimately result in a cruel hoax for many workers in the enterprise.

Improving the Portability of Pension Entitlements

The U.S. economy has benefited from a highly mobile labor force with most workers changing jobs many times throughout their working lives. There is every indication that as the structure of the economy continues to change, high rates of labor mobility will continue as workers move to jobs in which their productivity is greatest. Pension policy can contribute to overall productivity growth if pension entitlements can be easily transferred from one job to another so that worker mobility is increased. If pension benefits were more easily transferred from one job to another, the value of pension benefits on retirement would, on average, be significantly higher—perhaps twice as high as current benefit levels.

Except in the college world, the goal of complete portability has proved elusive, and indeed complete portability may discourage the establishment of new pension plans. Earlier vesting does provide partial portability, but I think we can attempt to extend the concept even further.

As part of future policy changes we should consider introducing disincentives for employees who decide to cash out entitlements to a defined benefit prior to retirement. Similarly, we should discourage lump-sum benefit distributions from defined-contribution plans.

Penalizing cash distributions has been resisted by both employer and employee groups, and government regulation of this feature of employer-based plans raises difficult issues since the reinvestment of the lump sum can, if interest rates are high, yield a greater return if the cash distribution is reinvested by the worker. All the evidence, however, indicates that for most workers lump-sum cash distributions are not reinvested. Based on this experience, I personally favor an additional tax penalty on lump-sum benefit distributions that are not rolled over into an IRA or some form of annuity.

If business is prepared to advocate tax incentives to encourage employers and employees to establish and contribute to pension plans for retirement income, business groups should also be prepared to support policies which ensure that the benefits are actually used to improve the ability of employer-based pensions to provide income throughout the retiree's remaining life.

Conclusions

I have tried to provide you with a businessman's perspective on the important policy issues concerning the future role of pensions within our retirement income system. Strengthening the future role of employer pensions will not be achieved by tinkering with ERISA regulations. If you believe as I do that in the long run less reliance on Social Security and more reliance on pensions for retirement income are essential to future productivity growth, then labor, business, and policymakers must concentrate their efforts on the really important issues of pension policy reform. These issues include increasing pension coverage.

As I have indicated, providing pension credits for workers who continue to work past 65 years of age will not increase coverage in any significant way. Employers who wish to provide such coverage should, of course, be free to do so, and many have moved in this direction. For workers in some industries, mandatory coverage requirements would be counterproductive since it would raise the cost of continuing to employ older workers. Similarly, I believe we have to be flexible on coverage of part-time workers, especially those with short tenure.

Employees in small firms are potentially the most important source of greater participation in employer plans. To encourage increased participation among this group of workers, I have suggested an approach which involves worker participation in the decision on whether or not to establish an employer-based plan. Together, workers and employers should consider the advantages and disadvantages of taking part of employee compensation in the form of saving for retirement. For some workers a pension plan will not be an attractive option, especially if they do not expect to be vested in the plan. Earlier vesting, or a 401(k) type of plan will, however, make pensions more attractive to employees in small firms.

The second critical issue for the long-run role of pensions is how to transfer pension entitlement from one job to another. Earlier vesting is a way of increasing the portability of pension entitlement, but it is only a partial solution. It is also evident that we must consider ways to discourage employees from using lump-sum distributions of pension entitlement for purposes other than their future retirement income.

While I hope the ideas and proposals I have outlined will help redirect the debate on pension issues, I am fully aware that I have presented no definitive solutions. But I do hope that the participants at the Pension Research Council conference will continue to be in the vanguard of developing a consensus on achieving these desirable goals.

Economic Security: The Employee's Perspective

by Robert D. Paul*

7

American democracy has developed a unique response to the challenge of providing economic security for its citizens. In the industrialized countries of Western Europe the government takes the major role in making sure that citizens have their incomes adequately replaced if they are unemployed, are disabled, or retire; the government also provides significant protection against the cost of medical and hospital care. In the United States the balance is quite different. There is individual responsibility, employer responsibility, and government responsibility.

How did this unique system develop? What are its strengths and weaknesses? What kind of economic security does it provide for our citizens? What threats does it face? What may lie ahead? These are the sorts of questions which this chapter will consider. The answers will help illuminate the current concerns of employees, particularly the younger employees as they assume positions of leadership and influence in the working world.

---

*Vice Chairman, Martin E. Segal & Company.

Historical Evolution

As America entered the 20th century, it was rapidly becoming an industrial nation, a nation with more employees and fewer self-employed farmers and artisans. Employers, especially those with a growing number of employees and an aging work force, began to be concerned about providing economic security for their workers after retirement. Many such employers were in the transportation business. Railroads, delivery companies, and shipping companies were prominent among those who at the end of the 19th century or early in the 20th decided that it was appropriate to sponsor a pension plan.

After World War I, pension programs began to spread to the steel, telephone, photographic, and other prospering industries. By the end of the 1920s, pension protection had spread to cover about 15 percent of the work force. The Depression ended all that. Most pension plans did not survive the Depression. The pension plans of the railroad industry were federalized and are still administered by the Railroad Retirement Board. The Social Security Act was passed in 1935, in part in reaction to the failing pension plans that were leaving people in destitution after a lifetime of work.

Earlier, laws had been passed that protected employees against the hazards of on-the-job injuries. These state workers' compensation laws have been expanded and strengthened, but they are still in force in all the states. The Depression also spawned a state and federal partnership to provide unemployment insurance.

During the Depression, increasing urbanization and the changing nature of medical care practice helped to create a demand for pre-paid hospital care. The Blue Cross movement was founded about 50 years ago to help fill that need. As the 1930s drew to a close and the economy gradually recovered, insurance to protect against the cost of doctors' bills became available to meet the demand for this additional protection.

World War II caused a rapid increase in all types of employee benefits. Employers adopted these benefit programs to help recruit employees to work in war factories. They were motivated as well by an excess-profits tax that encouraged employers to spend money on employees' needs rather than on taxes and by the exclusion of benefit costs from wage and price controls. In the years from 1941 to 1954, health, life, disability, and pension plans began to be more common throughout the economy.

Favorable tax treatment of benefit plans, originally enacted in 1921, was reinforced in 1942. It permitted tax deductions to companies for the cost of benefits, the accumulation of reserves for pension plans in a tax-sheltered environment, and the postponement of taxation to the employees until the benefits were paid out after retirement. Health insurance premiums and benefits were free of taxation. Group life insurance also received favorable tax treatment. Is it any wonder that insurance companies were growing and prospering by selling these new employee-benefit programs, almost all of which were insured?

By the end of World War II the social insurance programs, developed to bail out the fledgling private programs established in the 1920s, had been supplemented by programs adopted during the war in a kind of hodgepodge way. Industrial unions, which had been formed near the end of the 1930s, saw benefit programs as an important priority in early postwar bargaining. Health insurance and pension programs were negotiated throughout all of unionized industry after a leading court case made it clear that they were a proper subject for collective bargaining.

After the war, several states expanded social legislation by adopting disability benefits laws that provided for continuation of a portion of wages in the event of nonoccupational illness or accident. Rhode Island, New Jersey, and New York on the East Coast adopted such laws; California, Hawaii, and Puerto Rico did so later. But the expectation that such laws would be adopted by all 50 states to parallel the workers' compensation laws has not been fulfilled. Unions, instead, bargained for these benefits, and employers, in turn, provided them for their salaried employees and nonunion employees in the form of salary-continuance programs.

The 25 years from 1950 to 1975 saw a steady expansion of both private employee benefits provided by employers and the Social Security system of the federal government. Employer-provided health, disability, and life insurance spread to cover 85 to 90 percent of the private work force. Pension protection spread to cover half the work force, perhaps two thirds of the work force over age 25, and as much as 85 percent of the work force employed by employers of 1,000 or more people. Thrift and savings plans that began in the oil industry spread to other industries. Supplemental unemployment insurance was negotiated in the more cyclical industries. Retirement ages dropped as capital was substituted for labor in more and more industries. Service pensions, borrowed from the military and the uniformed forces of local government, were adopted, adding to the language the term *30 and out*.

Nor were things quiet on the federal front. The taxable wage base for Social Security rose steadily. The percentage of the average wage replaced rose from about 25 percent in 1941 to just over 51 percent in 1980. It is now dropping back to about 41 percent of the average wage and is scheduled to remain there for the foreseeable future. Disability benefits were added to the program. Retirement was permitted as early as age 62 on an actuarially reduced basis. Benefits were indexed to cost-of-living changes. Most revolutionary of all, insurance against the cost of hospital and medical care for retirees 65 or older was included as part of the Social Security system in the middle 1960s. Medicare for retired workers was supplemented by Medicaid, the state-federal partnership to provide medical care for the medically indigent. Both were enacted partly in response to the wave of interest in a national health insurance program for all Americans which peaked about that time.

The parallel growth of various forms of economic security in both the private sector and through the Social Security system was reinforced by the widespread growth in home ownership of those who returned from the war to marry and raise families in the suburbs. Capital was also substituted for labor at home. Washing machines, dryers, vacuum cleaners, refrigerators, stereos, TVs, and an endless variety of durable goods have transformed the way work and leisure is experienced in the American home. Home ownership also represents a store of savings that can be liquidated in retirement to provide income as a supplement to Social Security and employer-sponsored pension plans.

By the mid-1970s, employer-sponsored pension plans came under attack. Some said there should be mandatory vesting. Others wanted more rapid actuarial funding and insurance against the termination of a pension plan by an employer who was no longer able to continue to fund it. There were cries for fuller disclosure of the terms of the pension plan, fiduciary standards for those who invest their assets, and portability of benefit rights. Many of these provisions were incorporated in a law, now known as ERISA. That was the beginning of what can now be called the regulatory era in the employee benefits field.

Current Scenario

These new concerns have to do with issues of equity and fairness. They include benefit limitations, mandatory surviving spouses' benefits, minimum benefits for smaller employers who have a large percentage of highly paid executives, and earlier vesting for employees of smaller employers. Nondiscrimination standards are gradually being introduced for health and life insurance programs.

While the federal government is cutting back on Medicare and shifting the cost to employers, it is not allowing the prefunding of postretirement health and life insurance. Integration with Social Security is gradually being eroded; changes have already been made in relation to long-term disability benefits. Tax policy now favors using insurance companies to underwrite certain kinds of benefits out of fear that otherwise employers will establish reserves in self-insured trust funds for tax avoidance reasons rather than properly fund for the expected benefit payments. Individual retirement accounts (IRA) are encouraged, while taxation of some part of the health insurance package is proposed. Employee ownership of companies is encouraged by legislation permitting employee stock ownership plans (ESOP), while employee ownership of company stock through matching contributions to 401(k) salary-reduction contributions may soon be discouraged or perhaps eliminated.

Prospects for the Future

The compact between the federal government and the private sector that helped to create a growing private-sector role and a diminishing responsibility for the federal government is now in considerable jeopardy. It may be sacrificed to the deficit reducers who are not ready to tackle their real job or to the tax reformers who may inadvertently make private employee-benefit programs so difficult to administer that employers will throw up their hands and let Uncle Sam do it.

Employees do not want that to happen. They are worried about the future of Social Security. They are not sure that the intergenerational transfer mechanism can survive the bulge of the baby boom and the inability of the system to continue to deliver much more in benefits than individual employees have paid in payroll taxes. The work force is better educated than ever, more women are working, and there are more two-earner families. Can the Social Security system in its present form continue to meet the needs of this changing work force?

Employees prefer the flexibility that private-sector plans have allowed. They want to be able to choose from a variety of benefits. Early in their careers they may want more cash to buy the furniture and cars and other durable goods they need when they are first starting out. Later they need life insurance, disability insurance, a way to save to meet the needs of later life, such as buying a house or paying school tuition, a way to pay for child care, or perhaps to obtain legal services, or to buy auto or homeowners insurance at a reasonable price. Still later they become concerned with retirement income and how they might invest their capital after retirement.

No government program can meet these life-cycle needs as effectively as programs developed by employers for their own work forces. Nor can any government program do it as cost effectively as it can be done in the private sector. Employees want the partnership between the federal government and employers to be continued and strengthened. They want private sector plans to become the senior partner because they have more faith that the funded programs in the private sector will deliver what is promised. They certainly want Social Security continued and kept financially secure. They also want the government to encourage savings and individual initiative. Our country has the lowest savings rate among the industrial democracies. Other countries encourage savings through their tax system. We are considering cutting back sharply our encouragement of savings through tax-deferred employee-benefit programs.

What employees want most is a government that helps to nurture a growing economy. The most important element of economic security is a decent job for as long as you want to hold one. Meeting that objective and making our country more competitive in the world economy means coping with the current fiscal disarray.

After the above, the wish list of most employees might include:

1. Development of a national retirement income and employee benefits policy that spells out the roles of the government, employers, and individuals.
2. A period of no further legislative and regulatory changes following the adoption of a national policy to permit the private sector to develop appropriate programs and to operate them without change for a number of years.
3. A reaffirmation of the compact between the federal government and employers so that the progress made since World War II in enlarging the economic security of the average American can be continued.
4. Consideration of changes in the Social Security system to make it more responsive to the needs of today's and tomorrow's work force.
5. A method to encourage development of plans for employees whose employers do not yet sponsor plans, particularly in smaller companies and lower-paying industries.
6. A way to encourage the private sector to fund health insurance for retired workers so that a better balance between federal and private programs can develop.

America has built the most prosperous society ever to inhabit the earth. The prosperity can be continued by an enlightened continuing partnership between the private sector and the federal government, one which allows ample room for individuals to make a contribution to their own economic security. The challenge is again before us. Will we respond as effectively in the 1980s and 1990s as we did in the 1950s and 1960s?

Pension Industry: What Role?

8

by George B. Swick*

"It was a strange beast created by American society—lived for a few years, but didn't adjust to a new climate."

Source: Buck Consultants, Inc. Reprinted from *Dun's Review*, September 1980. Used with permission.

As Chairman of Buck Consultants, Inc., I selected the above cartoon as the basis for one of our first public advertisements. In the absence of text, it appears to forecast the ultimate demise of

---

*Retired chairman, George B. Buck Consulting Actuaries, Inc.

pension programs in the United States. In actual fact, the cartoon was not intended to sound a death knell, but rather to caution that, absent imaginative and intelligent approaches, private pension programs might well disappear, or be forced to disappear.

My personal opinion is that, if pension programs did not exist, they would have to be invented, so long as the United States continues to encourage a market-oriented, capitalistic economy.

When individuals, through voluntary desire, social desire, incapacity, or economic dislocation are unwilling or unable to participate in active productivity, some means beyond after-tax personal savings must be found to meet the postemployment needs of income, capital accumulation, health care, and survivor benefits.

Federal, state, and local programs of welfare and "transfer" payments (Social Security, Medicare, unemployment compensation, etc.) provide a necessary and important floor, but cannot provide a "quality of life" acceptable to most citizens by themselves. Thus, an extensive system of supplemental retirement programs is an essential element for our social and economic system.

Absent the taxation powers of the federal, state, and local governmental welfare and "transfer" programs, there is no underwriting alternative to the accumulation of reserves during active employment to meet these postemployment requirements.

Whatever the nature of these programs, four essential goals must be met:

1. Accommodate the needs of human resources.
2. Accommodate the appropriate role of the employer (government, voluntary, or private sector).
3. Maintain the financial soundness of the programs.
4. Maintain the economic incentive of the sponsor to remain a viable funding source.

Whatever the nature of these programs, meeting the goals through the concept of an orderly accumulation of reserves would seem to require the same skills as those involved at present: namely, expertise in accounting concepts, actuarial concepts, administration, finance, human resource planning, investment, legal, legislative, underwriting, and the like.

We have developed a unique system in the United States. It is large, complex, and perhaps somewhat inefficient, but it does exist, it does operate, and it does adapt to a changing social and economic environment.

Obviously, Social Security and private pension plans provide only two elements of the total financial resources available to the elderly. A complete list would include the following:

- Welfare.
- Social Security.
- Medicare.
- Qualified pension plans.
    - Defined benefit.
    - Defined contribution.
- Nonqualified pension plans and deferred compensation.
- Employer-provided supplemental health-care coverage.
- Employer-provided life insurance.
- Personal savings.
- Personal supplemental health-care coverage.
- Personal life insurance.
- Part-time (or full-time) employment.
- Personal tax incentives:
    - Individual Retirement Accounts.
    - Salary-reduction plans (Internal Revenue Code Section 401(k)).
    - Employer-provided health care.
    - Ten-year averaging of lump-sum pension settlements.

While all of the above factors are of interest, the primary focus of this chapter remains the private "qualified" pension system. Some reflections upon employer-provided health-care coverage will be included later on, however, because the availability, or lack thereof, may well become a major force in the retirement decision-making process.

Early Growth of Pension Plans in the United States[1]

The first pension plan in the United States was established by New York City in 1859, covering its policemen. The first plan in industry was the American Express Company plan in 1875. Another significant year was 1905 when the Granite Cutters established the first trade union (multiemployer) plan. All these plans, as well as all other plans established before 1917, were funded on a pay-as-you-go basis. No reserves were established from contributions of the plan sponsors. If a plan sponsor became insolvent or terminated the plan, the pension payments generally stopped and all benefits were lost.

Some of the early plans required employee contributions, in which case these amounts were accumulated in employees' accounts. However, it took 58 years from the establishment of the first pension plan to the establishment of the first funded plan in the United States. The first plan established on a funded basis for both the employees' and the employer's money was the Teachers' Retirement System of the City of New York, which began operating in 1917. In 1921, the first insured group-annuity contract was issued by the Metropolitan Life Insurance Company of New York.

In 1935, the establishment of the federal Social Security system greatly expanded the idea of pension planning and created a floor of protection. Contributions were paid into the fund starting in 1937, although benefit payments did not begin until 1940. As a result, a fund was created from which benefits were paid. In the early days the fund and incoming contributions were sufficiently large to maintain the benefits on an actuarially sound basis. This, together with the fact that the official name of the Social Security Act is the Federal Insurance and Contribution Act, has led many people erroneously to view Social Security as insured and actuarially sound, and to expect a relationship between their contributions and expected benefits

[1]From paper presented at 1979 Employee Benefit Research Institute Forum, "Pension Plan Termination Insurance: Does the Foreign Experience Have Relevance in the United States?"

similar to the relationship between premiums and proceeds from an insurance company.

By 1940, the private pension system in the United States covered more than 4 million persons (out of a total population slightly more than 130 million), receiving annual benefits of $140 million. Pension reserves totaled $2.4 billion in 1940, one fifth of what they would be 10 years later.

There were two major causes of expansion in the private pension system in the 1940s. Inflation and taxation during World War II stimulated the expansion of private pension plans in industry. More that 2.25 million additional workers became covered by plans by 1945. The other major factor encouraging the spread of private pensions stemmed from collective bargaining. After World War II, many unions wanted to include pensions and other welfare benefits in the labor negotiation process. In a landmark decision, the United States Supreme Court ruled in 1949 (*Inland Steel Co.* v. *National Labor Relations Board)* that employers were required to bargain on the issue of pensions. Also in 1949, the Steel Industry Fact-Finding Board held that the steel industry had an obligation to provide its workers with pensions and other welfare benefits to take care of temporary and permanent depreciation of human machinery. From 1950 on, the unions have been an important factor in the spread and direction of pension coverage in the United States.

By 1950, more than 10 million persons (out of a total population in excess of 150 million) were covered under private pension plans. Pension reserves approached $12 billion and annual payments to beneficiaries totaled $370 million. Annual contributions to these plans exceeded $2 billion by 1950.

Recent Growth of Pension Plans in the United States

According to the American Council of Life Insurance[2] the greatest growth in private pension plans in terms of coverage, contributions, beneficiaries, benefit payments, and assets oc-

[2]*Pension Facts*, 1984/1985.

curred in the 1950s. Private plans covered 23 million persons and annual contributions reached $5.6 billion by year-end 1960. Reserves increased to $57 billion, and benefit payments totaled $1.7 billion.

The growth in contributions and benefits under private retirement plans slowed during the 1960s, and much of the growth that occurred was due to inflation. At year-end 1970, 36.1 million persons were covered by private pension plans, and contributions were $15 billion. Benefit payments amounted to $7.4 billion, and reserves reached $152 billion.

By year-end 1975, some 38.4 million active workers were covered by private pension plans, and contributions were about $32.2 billion. From 1970 to 1975, benefit payments more than doubled to $14.9 billion, and reserves increased by 71 percent to $259 billion.

A nationwide survey in May 1983 by the Employee Benefit Research Institute and the U.S. Department of Health and Human Services indicated that 56 percent of 88 million nonfarm workers in 1983 said they were covered under a private sector plan in 1983.[3] This represents a combined figure which breaks down into 83 percent of government (federal, state, and local) employees and 50 percent of nongovernment employees. Restricting the nonfarm workers population to those (1) between ages 25 and 65, (2) working 1,000 hours or more, and (3) working at the same job for at least one year, the 56 percent figure rises to 70 percent. With respect to those not covered, the Employee Benefit Research Institute Notes state as follows:

> Not everyone is covered by a retirement plan. Noncovered workers can be sorted into five categories. Fifteen percent of uncovered workers are self-employed, and appear to reinvest their savings in their own businesses instead of in traditional retirement plans. Three percent of uncovered workers are in agriculture. These workers are seasonal and have numerous other employment problems. Twenty-seven percent of uncovered workers are under age 25 or age 65 and over and thus do not meet participation requirements of the Employee Retirement Income Security Act (ERISA). Through the 1984 Retirement Equity Act (REA), which lowered the minimum participation age from 25 to 21, employers will now include 583,000 additional younger employees in their pension plans.

---

[3]Employee Benefit Research Institute Notes of May/June 1985.

Workers without coverage who did not meet ERISA's minimum service requirements, i.e., those who were on the job less than one year or who usually worked fewer than 1,000 hours, accounted for another 20 percent of all noncovered workers. Those who met 1983 ERISA participation and service standards (the "ERISA work force") made up the remaining 34 percent of all noncovered workers. But they only represent 16 percent of total employment.

Assets and reserves of major nonfederal pension and retirement programs in the United States have grown as follows:[4]

	Private-Sector Plans	*State and Local Employers ($000,000)*	*IRA and Keogh*
1960	$ 56,998	$ 19,600	N.A.
1970	151,569	58,200	N.A.
1980	578,504	185,226	N.A.
1983	872,352	289,731	$102,901

The rapid growth of the private retirement system over the past 30 years has been remarkable.

Equally remarkable, however, has been the adaptability of the system to concerns and issues raised from many directions. I doubt that any other system would have continued to grow, and even thrive, when confronted by so many forces.

Since my personal professional career began in 1949, it has paralleled the major period of growth and adaptability of the system. Hopefully, observations of the many issues which have confronted the system, and how it adapted, will clearly demonstrate the flexibility and adaptability of the private pension system and, perhaps, help establish directions for the future.

Disability

One of the first concerns in the 1950s was how to deal with disability income given the disastrous experience of the life insurance industry with respect to disability income riders during the 1930s. Tentative disability income benefits were added in the beginning, which have now evolved into fully integrated systems of short-term disability income benefits, followed by long-term disability income benefits with continued pension

[4] *Pension Facts*, 1984/1985.

accruals until age 65, at which point the retirement system takes over.

Survivor Benefits

Many early retirement systems were funded through life insurance policies with significant life insurance protection. Trusteed plans initially looked to group life insurance for such protection and contained no survivor benefits, other than optional settlements at retirement. During the 1960s, survivor benefits payable upon death in active service began to be added. The trend was formalized in 1974 under ERISA and further expanded by the Retirement Equity Act of 1984. Many programs provide these required preretirement survivor coverages at no cost to the participant, and some plans provide subsidized postretirement joint and survivor settlement options as well. Through ERISA and the Retirement Equity Act, Congress has made certain that the rights of survivors are fully recognized.

Vesting

Vesting in pension benefits has been, and continues to be, a major issue. Early programs had little or no vesting prior to eligibility for early retirement. During the 1960s and early 1970s, more liberal vested rights provisions were developing, primarily as a result of the collective bargaining process. Once again, vesting was formalized by ERISA in 1974, with safeguards that vested rights could not be circumvented through plan design (i.e., excessively increasing benefits for later periods of service).

The primary difficulty today is the lack of adjustment in benefits during the deferral period, the cost of which is generally considered unacceptable to employers. There is a modest trend developing, however, to settle such vested rights in a lump-sum distribution which can then be rolled over, on a tax-free basis, to an individual retirement account, putting the entire risk during the deferred period squarely upon the individual, similar to a defined contribution plan.

Inflation

During the 1970s, inflationary pressures became a major issue for pension systems.

During the pension accrual period, negotiated flat-benefit plans were bargained upwards retroactively, career pay plans were amended retroactively, and average final salary plans were adjusted automatically.

Benefits payable to current retirees were increased through the collective bargaining process, where applicable, even though the Supreme Court ruled that employers did not have to negotiate with respect to retirees. With respect to other retirees, many employers provided periodic ad hoc increases.

Little, if any, consideration was given to former employees with deferred vested rights. In addition, no consideration has been either given, or suggested, with respect to employees retired under a defined-contribution plan where the individual bears the entire risk.

Automatic adjustments were restricted, almost exclusively, to federal, state, and local programs, where taxing powers exist. Private employers were, and continue to be, reluctant to accept a cost which can be as high as 40 to 50 percent for an employee retiring at age 65 with annual increases of 5 percent per year. A few companies experimented with the development of schemes by which employees could transfer defined-contribution plan proceeds into a supplement to the defined-benefit plan with a proviso for specified annual increases in the defined-benefit pension. The recent declines in inflationary pressures have reduced the importance of this issue, but this may be only a temporary reprieve.

Coverage

Lack of coverage has been a constant issue. Supporters of the system point to the expansion of coverage, while detractors point to the continued lack of coverage along with the loss of benefits for those who switch jobs too frequently to meet vesting requirements.

ERISA established minimum participation rules where plans did exist, and these requirements were liberalized by the Retirement Equity Act. Neither act, however, requires the existence of a plan.

In addition, ERISA created the concept of a tax-deferred Individual Retirement Account, which was extended to all employed persons by the 1981 Economic Recovery Tax Act.

The Carter Commission on Pension Policy recommended a second tier of compulsory pension coverage to supplement Social Security. This proposal did not gain wide backing, although it does remain a possibility to fill the gap if the relative share of Social Security is forced by economic necessity to continue to decline.

Providing coverage for agricultural workers, part-time workers, and those at minimal wage levels, to supplement Social Security, does not appear practical, other than whatever use such individuals can make of Individual Retirement Accounts.

Benefit Security

Ever since the closing of Studebaker in 1963 there has been widespread concern over the safety of private defined-benefit pensions.

The Studebaker case exemplified the problem of funding private pensions. The plan had been amended two years prior to termination, with retroactive increases to both active and retired workers. The labor agreement required these increases to be funded over a period of 30 years, so that little funding was accomplished in the two-year period between the plan amendment and the termination. Furthermore, the labor agreement gave first priority on termination to retired employees, so that, upon termination, retired employees received full benefits (at the recently negotiated higher level), leaving little to be allocated to active employees.

Studebaker was not, and is not, an isolated case. Whenever a pension plan is amended retroactively, a funding gap is created which takes some time to be covered, as illustrated below.

Level of Past Service Benefit Funded over a Period of Time (based on 6 percent interest rate)

Years Elapsed	*Funding Period (Years)* 10	20	30
5	43%	15%	7%
10	100	36	17
15	100	63	29
20	100	100	47
30	100	100	100

Prior to ERISA, there was *no* statutory requirement to fund retroactively granted pension benefits. This situation was addressed by ERISA, but even under ERISA, minimum funding of retroactive benefit increase can be spread over as long as 30 years.

Thus, the fundamental funding gap remains. This funding gap was expected to be filled by Title IV of ERISA, with a five-year phase-in concept and maximum protected benefits, to protect the Pension Benefit Guaranty Corporation from selection against the system. Congress determined that the loss of pension benefits due to plan termination should not be borne solely by the employees involved, but should first be met from a charge against the plan sponsor, up to 30 percent of net worth, and then spread over all defined-benefit plans by a per capita annual charge.

Unfortunately, Congress did not adequately restrict the ability of a plan sponsor to terminate its pension plan, with a large uncovered obligation and minimal net worth. Nor did Congress provide safeguards where an employer was granted funding waivers due to poor economic conditions, while participants continued to accrue benefits covered by Title IV. Nor did Congress define a pension in terms of age; thus, if a plan pays full unreduced pensions at, say, age 55, the participants are fully protected, even though other plans require an actuarial reduction for pensions commencing as early as age 55 and are nevertheless required to pay equal per capita premiums. Not surprisingly, then, the per capita annual charge has increased from $1 to a potential of, perhaps, $8 in 1986 depending upon the mood of Congress.

Attempts have been made by the Pension Benefit Guaranty Corporation to achieve legislated changes in Title IV to protect the system from unjustified terminations, without success as yet. In addition, the Pension Benefit Guaranty Corporation has recently initiated a claim for damages, charging that an actuarial firm did not adequately forecast the financial impact of involuntary early retirement when determining the minimum funding requirements under ERISA. However, no consideration has been given (1) to adding a definition of when a pension is a "pension" in order to safeguard the program and to provide equity between plans with differing retirement ages, nor (2) to strengthening the amendment phase-in provisions.

Withdrawal Liability

Benefit security was of primary importance in the enactment of the concept of "withdrawal liability" for multiemployer pension plans in the Multi-Employer Pension Plans Amendment Act of 1980.

Prior to this statute, many employers did not concern themselves with the benefit security of multiemployer plans, under the theory that their sole financial commitment was to contribute in accordance with collective bargaining agreements.

The 1980 act created an adversarial relationship between employers terminating participation and those remaining, with the result that all employers became much more aware of the quality of funding under these plans. The result was, I believe, short-term aggravation, arbitration, and litigation, but long-term benefit to all, with both management and labor paying much more attention to the quality of funding under multiemployer plans.

Sex Discrimination

In the early days, many pension plans provided normal retirement for females five years earlier than for males. These differentials generally disappeared in the 1960s, accelerated by a number of court cases charging age discrimination.

During the legislative process leading up to the enactment of the 1965 Civil Rights Act, opponents added "sex" discrimination in an attempt to defeat the entire bill. The movement failed and "sex" remained in the bill. Senator Humphrey stated that the inclusion of "sex" was not to refer to retirement plans; however, this caveat was not included in the final language of the statute. During the process of awakening women's rights issues, the requirements for unequal contributions to provide equal benefits and the conversion of equal lump sums to unequal annuities became a major issue, and continue to be a major issue with respect to other forms of insurance-related products.

Several court cases were entered based upon the 1965 Civil Rights Act, with the latest resolution decided by the United States Supreme Court in 1983 in the *Norris* case, requiring equal treatment with respect to payments from a pension plan with respect to contributions made after August 1, 1983. This resolution ends with the payment of equal lump-sum amounts within the parameters of the plan itself with no restriction, as yet, on the use of sex-based mortality rates by insurance companies to sell individual annuity contracts outside of the plan to the recipients of such equalized lump-sum settlements.

The second primary issue in the *Norris* case was retroactivity, since retroactivity would, presumably, have required all accrued benefits, whether applicable to a male or female, to be raised to the highest level. This difficult issue was effectively compromised by creating the basic philosophy, but without retroactivity. Interestingly, there was no great actuarial issue, nor cost issue, in converting to unisex mortality rates on a prospective basis.

The basic issues are illustrated below:

I. Conversion of $10,000 Lump Sum Investment Plan Accumulation to Monthly Life Income

Age	*Male*	*Female*
60	$ 83.41	$ 75.10
65	93.27	81.55
70	107.18	91.24

II. Single-Premium $10,000 Life Insurance

60	$2,508	$1,677

III. 100% Joint and Survivor Pension Equivalent to $1,000 Per Annum Life Pension

	Male Pensioner with Female Contingent Annuitant	*Female Pensioner with Male Contingent Annuitant*
65	$ 740	$ 890

It is readily apparent that the use of unisex mortality rates provides both positive and negative results for those of each sex.

Another issue of major interest to women was the inclusion, in the 1984 Retirement Equity Act, of a specified statutory authority to recognize pension rights in legal separations and divorce actions.

Social Security Integration

The integration of private pensions around Social Security benefits has always been a controversial subject. The feeling of many is that tax incentives should not be given for programs which in some way offset a portion of Social Security benefits. Integration has been achieved through three different approaches: (1) direct offset; (2) lower percentage on Social Security covered earnings and higher percentage on the excess; or (3) indirect integration by establishing a nonintegrated formula with full recognition of the availability of Social Security.

The Social Security tax base for 1985 is $39,600, while the maximum earnings base for old-age benefits commencing in 1985 is approximately $23,000, yielding a maximum annual benefit determined as follows:

First	$ 3,360 × 90% =	$3,024	
Second	$16,932 × 32% =	5,418	
Balance	$ 2,708 × 15% =	406	
Total		$8,848	($737 per month)

The concept of Social Security integration merely attempts to provide larger total benefits for higher-paid employees, while still providing a lower total replacement ratio. For example, given a private pension formula of (1) 1 percent of Social Security covered earnings, and (2) 1.5 percent of the excess, an employee might be considered to accrue the following percentage of average earnings during a five-year period (1985–1989) from Social Security and the private pension combined:

Average Earnings	*Social Security Plus Private Pension as Percentage of Average Earnings*
$20,000	11.0
40,000	8.3
60,000	8.0
80,000	7.9

Up until 1985, Social Security benefits have received more favorable tax treatment than private pensions. In each case, employee contributions (or taxes) *are not* deductible for federal income tax purposes, while employer contributions (or taxes) *are* fully deductible. Until 1985, Social Security benefits were fully tax free, while pensions were taxed as ordinary income except for the portion deemed to be attributable to employee contributions. One-half of Social Security is now taxed as ordinary income if income exceeds specified levels. Thus, the tax incentive argument against integration by private programs does not appear to be supportable, nor does it invalidate the accomplishment of an acceptably balanced program from both sources.

Early Retirement

During the 1970s, and continuing into the 1980s, there has been a significant trend toward the reduction, or elimination, of actuarial reductions due to age for employees retiring before normal retirement age with variously specified age and/or service requirements. In some cases, a supplementary monthly pension is added, payable until age 65, or age 62, when old-age Social Security benefits are deemed to be first available.

The trend began in industry through the collective bargaining process, although uniformed firemen and policemen under state and local pension plans have had unreduced earlier retirement benefits since the inception of such plans. These benefits have greatly eased the burden of plant closings or permanent layoffs for older workers in many of the so-called smokestack industries. They have also formed a valuable basis upon which to build early retirement incentive programs for employers faced with the economic necessity to reduce the work force and who desire to do so in as humane a manner as possible. Finally, there are many employees with long periods of service who do wish to retire voluntarily at earlier ages.

There is a cost, however, and it is significant. Under a flat benefit plan, if the cost index for an employee working until age 65 and retiring on normal retirement equals 100, the cost index for unreduced early retirement at age 60 is about 160, while at age 55 it is about 240. These indices *do not* include the cost impact of supplementary pensions payable until old-age Social Security benefits are considered to be available.

Since unreduced early retirement benefits have been deemed covered by the insurance program of Title IV of ERISA, these same cost indices have added significantly to the emerging cost of the insurance program.

Mandatory Retirement Age

The Age Discrimination in Employment Act of 1978 took the system in exactly the opposite direction from unreduced early retirement benefits. This legislation has been supplemented by many state statutes prohibiting mandatory retirement at any age.

There are three alternative approaches to deferral of normal retirement beyond normal retirement age, generally established at age 65. The three approaches and their cost indices (related to an index of 100 at age 65), based upon retirement at age 70 are as follows:

1. Freeze benefits at age 65 with no further accruals (cost index of 65);
2. Continue to accrue benefits under the regular plan formula based on service and compensation until actual retirement (cost index of 75);
3. Provide retirement benefits with an actuarial value equal to that based upon retirement at normal retirement age (cost index of 100).

The Equal Employment Opportunities Commission is currently studying whether the first alternative should continue to be allowed. In any event, deferred retirement can only reduce cost, or continue the same cost, the exact opposite of subsidized early retirement benefits.

Early Retirement Incentive Plans

As previously indicated, a number of employers have designed one-time early retirement incentive programs in order to reduce their work force in as painless a manner as possible. In each case, employees elect to retire, if they wish, within a specified, limited, period of time. Additional benefits are payable in the form of (1) severance pay; (2) continued compensation for a limited period, (3) supplemental pensions until age 62 or age 65; (4) supplemental pensions for life; or (5) additional years of pension credit determined under the standard formula, etc.

Any supplemental pension benefits are usually paid outside of the formal "tax-qualified" program, with no funds accumulated and with tax deductions taken as benefits are paid. It should also be noted that employers have usually found that some continuance of employer-paid health-care coverage during retirement is essential to the success of the program. These programs can be expensive, but they are generally designed so that the reduction in labor cost due to the reduced work force will recover the added cost within a foreseeable limited period of time. While these early retirement incentive programs are not basic to the private retirement system, they do indicate how the system can be supplemented to meet social and economic conditions, just as they were supplemented in the area of involuntary layoff in some industries through collective bargaining.

Effect of Corporate Financial Statements

During the 1960s, the financial community became concerned about what pension obligations might exist beyond the assets of the plan, and about whether pension-expense flexibility created unacceptable differentials in earnings.

In 1965, the Accounting Principles Board adopted *Opinion No. 8*, which placed minimal restrictions on pension expense and which added financial statement disclosure of the unfunded value of vested benefits.

The Financial Accounting Standards Board has been studying this issue for several years, and has recently issued an Exposure Draft of a new Statement which would: (1) significantly narrow differentials in pension expense (but not differentials in actual funding); (2) add an "accounting liability" to the corporate balance sheet based upon accrued pension obligations; and (3) add disclosure to help the financial community analyze the funding levels and resulting expense charges. Many questions have arisen about the Exposure Draft, and the preceding deliberations, as to what impact such a Statement will have on (1) plan design, (2) funding policies, and (3) investment policies. Such questions include:

1. Will companies with final average salary plans be disadvantaged as compared with flat benefit plans or career pay plans?
2. Will narrowing of pension expense flexibility also narrow differentials in levels of pension funding?
3. Will companies shift pension reserves from externally invested assets to corporate balance sheet obligations?

Certainly, the pension system will survive, and adapt to, any such statement. However, plan sponsors will undoubtedly react in different ways until some preferred pattern emerges.

Funding Adequacy

Over the past 30 years, a massive financial institution has been created. The term "financial" does not mean "assets" alone. It can just as readily mean obligations (or liabilities, if you wish). Whether funded, over-funded, or under-funded is, perhaps, in the eye of the beholder.

As previously indicated, prior to the enactment of ERISA, there was no statutory nor regulatory requirement to fund pension benefits granted on a retroactive basis. Even with the enactment of minimum funding provisions under ERISA, there can be a long-term funding gap before retroactive benefit increases become fully covered by assets. These comments pertain particularly to flat benefit plans and career-pay plans.

Plans based upon average final pay present a quite different funding picture. With the ERISA requirements for reasonable actuarial assumptions, it is expected that assumptions with respect to future compensation levels will be employed. As a result, the situation often exists where assets exceed those required to fully fund benefits accrued to date (without projections for future compensation levels).

Reversion of Assets

Pension plans with funding ratios in excess of 100 percent have not escaped the eyes of the financial community and corporate raiders.

A number of financial managers now look at retirement plans as financial resources with, perhaps, only minimal concern for human resource security requirements. As a result, we see: (1) reversion of "perceived" excess pension assets, (2) use of "perceived" excess pension assets to reduce debt following a leveraged buyout, (3) spin-offs to avoid pension termination obligations, and (4) conversion of retirement income plans to employee stock ownership plans purely to accomplish leveraged buyouts. Federal regulations permit the reversion of excess assets provided all accrued benefits (vested and nonvested), without recognition of future pay increases, are laid off under an insured group annuity contract. Future benefit accruals can then be provided by reconstituting the same plan, switching to a defined-contribution plan, or even switching to an employee stock-ownership plan.

This is a controversial practice which has been highly criticized by members of Congress and others. Nevertheless, it has become a common practice where the recapture of excess assets is considered financially desirable for current management or a successful corporate raider. Elimination of such reversions by federal statute would not end the practice, but would give preference to the corporate raider who could still combine its own existing "under-funded" plan with the acquired plan with "excess" assets.

Obviously, if the same plan is reconstituted, future pension expenses charges and funding requirements will be higher (perhaps significantly higher) than if the reversion of assets had not taken place.

Investment in Employer Securities

One of the more interesting features of ERISA is the provision related to investing pension assets in securities of the plan sponsor. Prior to ERISA, many profit-sharing plans provided for investment in employer stock. Under thrift/savings plan arrangements, in many cases the employer's matching contributions were invested in employer stock or an option to invest in employer stock was available. Under defined-benefit plans, most employers did not invest in employer securities, except as the result of investing in a pooled fund arrangement. On the other hand, some employers invested rather heavily in employer securities within the rather loose regulatory framework in place.

ERISA then placed a 10 percent limitation with respect to defined-benefit plans, with no limits on defined-contribution plans. Thus, where the employer (or, perhaps, ultimately the PBGC) is at risk, investment in employer securities is restricted. Where the employee is solely at risk, on the other hand, there is no such restriction.

During the early 1980s, with deteriorating economic conditions and cash flow problems, a number of employers, who had never invested in employer securities within defined-benefit plans, revisited the ERISA provisions and decided the 10 percent clause was not so much a "limitation" as an "invitation." These employers contributed large amounts of employer securities in lieu of cash contributions, while remaining within the limitation of 10 percent of total assets.

Given the significant balance-sheet reserves established to cover pension benefits for plant closings, the reversion of assets, the possible results of expensing versus funding decisions of the Financial Accounting Standards Board, and the lack of tax-exempt funding opportunities for postretirement health-care coverages, we may well see a significant build up in balance-sheet reserves. These reserves are, of course, essentially the same as employer securities, although no priority status in bankruptcy is specifically provided. Those who propose limitations on external funding arrangements would do well to consider the alternatives from the perspective of employee security.

Defined Benefits versus Defined Contributions

Perhaps the most intriguing issue today is that of defined-benefit plans versus defined-contribution plans.

From the employee's perspective, the advantages of a defined-benefit plan, and thus the disadvantages of a defined-contribution plan, are as follows:

1. Specific retirement income goals can be established.
2. Early retirement benefits in excess of reduced actuarial equivalents can be achieved.
3. Postretirement cost-of-living adjustments, while not guaranteed, can be anticipated in times of severe inflation.
4. ERISA Title IV guarantees are available.
5. There is no loss of benefits due to poor investment performance.

From the opposite perspective, the advantages of a defined-contribution plan, and thus the disadvantages of a defined-benefit plan, are as follows:

1. There is an individual account balance to be perceived.
2. There is, generally, faster vesting.

3. Defined-contribution plans are often easier to understand.
4. Added benefits accrue to participants from good investment performance.
5. In some cases, loans are available during employment.
6. Funds can be portable on termination of employment.

Table 8–1 illustrates some of these advantages, or disadvantages, depending upon the viewer's perspective.

Turning to the employer, the advantages of a defined-benefit plan, and thus the disadvantages of a defined-contribution plan, are as follows:

1. Specific retirement income goals can be established.
2. There is flexibility of funding.

Table 8–1

Examples of Defined Benefits and Defined Contributions (hired age 35 at $20,000 increasing 5 percent per year, dollar amounts in thousands)

Retirement Age	*Preretirement Pay*	*Defined benefit (1¼% × Average final pay × Service)*	*Defined Contribution (6%)*	
			Investment Income at 5% per Year	
		Pension	*Lump Sum*	*Equivalent Pension*
60	64.5	18.3 (28%)*	96.8	8.6 (13%)
65	82.3	28.1 (34%)	148.2	14.8 (18%)
70	105.1	41.8 (40%)†	220.7	25.2 (24%)
			Investment Income at 8% per Year	
60	64.5	18.3 (28%)*	138.5	12.5 (19%)
65	82.3	28.1 (34%)	229.7	23.0 (28%)
70	105.1	41.8 (40%)†	370.8	42.4 (40%)
			Investment Income at 10% per Year	
60	64.5	18.3 (28%)*	178.8	16.0 (25%)
65	82.3	28.1 (34%)	315.0	31.5 (38%)
70	105.1	41.8 (40%)†	542.0	61.9 (59%)

Social Security adds 20–40%.

*No early retirement reduction.
†Continued pay and service accruals after age 65.

3. Usually there is a slower vesting.
4. Investment income gains reduce the employer's cost.

Again, from the opposite side, the disadvantages of a defined-benefit plan, and thus the advantages of a defined-contribution plan, are as follows:

1. Unfunded past service obligations must be recognized.
2. ERISA Title IV premiums, of unknown future proportions, are required, along with a potential call on net worth.
3. There is an uncertain cost element in the area of early retirement.
4. There is the potential for postretirement adjustments for inflation.
5. Investment income losses increase the employer's cost.

Not surprisingly, the issue has attained the attention of Congress. The history of the congressional action, beginning with the enactment of ERISA, appears to favor defined-contribution plans. While one might wish that Congress would be more neutral, it is not surprising given the problems Congress has been forced to deal with in the area of defined-benefit plans: (1) problems of comprehension; (2) problems of lack of vesting; (3) problems created by past service obligations; (4) problems created by ERISA Title IV; and (5) problems of postretirement inflation indexation.

While all of these issues are equally inherent (if not visibly so) in defined-contribution plans, Congress has taken a number of major steps to encourage capital accumulation programs, both individually and employer-provided: (1) individual retirement accounts, (2) employee stock ownership plans, (3) salary reduction plans (Internal Revenue Code Section 401(k)), (4) lower maximum limits on defined benefit plans, and (5) favorable tax treatment of lump sum settlements through 10-year averaging and IRA rollovers.

Nevertheless, both employers and employees seem to feel a mutual objective in the ability to establish specific retirement income goals for at least a basic level of retirement income. Thus, the role of defined-benefit plans should remain secure.

Table 8–2 illustrates an example of a combined program with the employee contributing 4 percent of pay, taking advantage of IRC Section 401(k) salary reduction.

Table 8–2

Example of Combined Program of Defined Benefit and Defined Contribution (hired age 35 at $20,000 increasing 5 percent per year, dollar amounts in thousands)

Retirement Age	*Preretirement Pay*	*Defined benefit (1% × Average final pay × Service)*	*Defined Contribution (4% Employee Salary Reduction, 2% Employer Match)*	
			Investment Income at 5% per Year	
		Pension	*Lump Sum*	*Equivalent Pension*
60	64.5	14.7 (23%)*	96.8	8.6 (12%)
65	82.3	22.5 (27%)	148.2	14.8 (18%)
70	105.1	33.4 (32%)†	220.7	25.2 (24%)
			Investment Income at 8% per Year	
60	64.5	14.7 (23%)*	138.5	12.5 (19%)
65	82.3	22.5 (27%)	229.7	23.0 (28%)
70	105.1	33.4 (32%)†	370.8	42.4 (40%)
			Investment Income at 10% per Year	
60	64.5	14.7 (23%)*	178.8	16.0 (25%)
65	82.3	22.5 (27%)	370.8	31.5 (38%)
70	105.1	33.4 (32%)†	542.0	61.9 (59%)

Social Security adds 20–40%.

*No early retirement reduction.
†Continued pay and service accruals after age 65.

Lump Sum Settlements

Tax incentives, and the relatively high "real" interest rates of recent years, have led to media attention to the advantages of lump-sum pension distributions from defined-benefit plans, along with tax-free preretirement borrowing from defined-contribution plans.

In the early days, many plans were funded through ordinary life insurance contracts, under which lump-sum settlements, equal to the cash value of the policies, were the norm. As plans moved toward trusteed-funding vehicles, some plans retained, or added, lump-sum settlements but only where the individual could demonstrate the availability of other assets along with a clear tax advantage. These restrictions have disappeared along with other so-called discriminatory practices.

As the demand increased, employers came to realize that lump-sum settlements had to be determined at current investment income rates of return, rather than the lower actuarial assumed rate of investment return used for future funding purposes. Otherwise, the plan suffers a true financial loss. The assumptions most often used are the current rates used by the Pension Benefit Guaranty Corporation, those reflected by intermediate government bonds, or by published corporate bond indexes. This change took some of the glamour off lump-sum settlements, but the tax advantages of "10-year averaging" and pre-1974 capital gains treatment remain.

In my opinion, lump-sum settlements of defined benefits should be offered only after careful consideration by the employer, particularly if a companion defined-contribution plan exists.

Demographic Trends

While many factors have been directly influencing the emergence of the pension system, indirect forces from changing demographics are also occurring. Increasing life expectancies are well known. However, it is less well known that increases in life expectancy for those actually reaching retirement age is a recent development.

According to mortality studies of corporate retirees, the typical man of 65 can now expect to live beyond 80, and a woman of 65 will survive on average to almost 85. The comparable figures as recently as 15 years ago for men and women were 78.5 and 83, respectively. Moreover, this significant increase in life expectancy appeared only in the last 5 to 10 years, which may portend even greater longevity for retirees in the immediate future.

The impact on both Social Security and the private pension system is obvious. The basic question is whether some of the increase in life expectancies should be added to productive years, rather than merely added to extend retirement years. Social Security has already been revised in 1983 to increase the normal retirement age to age 66 by the year 2009 (i.e., those born in 1943 and later), and to age 67 by the year 2027 (i.e., those born in 1960 and later).

No similar trend has appeared in the private pension system, although the Age Discrimination in Employment Act may turn out effectively to accomplish the same result through individual, voluntary, action by employees. The dichotomy is that we have pressures building for both earlier and later retirement within the private pension system, at the same time as Social Security moves solely in the direction of later retirement.

As previously indicated, the timing of retirement is, perhaps, the most critical area of cost within the pension system. The way in which the system has developed to date effectively leaves the control of retirement in the hands of individual decision making. In addition to demographic shifts, one must also recognize the lifestyle trends leading to increases in the number of single households, single-parent families, and dual workers, along with a rise in part-time and self-employment.

Forces of Retirement

Before rushing into major changes in the retirement decision-making process, we need to know more about the forces involved.

Certainly, early retirements due to plant closings, involuntary layoffs, and other adverse economic factors will continue to pressure the private sector to provide relief through the early-retirement process. Interestingly, Social Security has not been subjected to social pressure in this direction, with the exception of disability.

Some will argue that the decision with respect to voluntary retirement is related exclusively to economics. If the employee feels his prospect for retirement income, from all sources, is reasonably satisfactory, that person will in fact retire.

The experience under the Age Discrimination in Employment Act has not as yet developed in any meaningful way. There appear to be some indications with respect to early-retirement incentive plans that long-service employees are more likely to retire than short-service employees. However, this may merely reflect the fact that long-range pension benefits are more likely to be higher for those with longer periods of service.

Placing the primary focus on defined-contribution plans and

personal savings through tax incentives would seem to lead directly to deferral of the retirement decision (see Table 8–1). Whether this is a desirable goal might, however, be seriously questioned.

There is a definite need for research in this area, by analyzing retirement trends and by surveying those who have retired and those who have not. The Policy Center on Aging at the Heller Graduate School of Brandeis University has done some work in this area, but it is only a beginning and time is running out. The aging of the baby-boom generation will mean that half of the working population will be between ages 35 and 55 by the year 2000. By the year 2010, a major segment of the working population will be within the period of retirement decision making.

It would appear that we will need an extraordinarily flexible system capable of accommodating all of the retirement forces which may be expected to arise from the aging of the baby-boom generation. This flexibility will not occur within the Social Security system, which leaves the entire burden on the private pension system and personal savings. Since personal savings provide a larger income source if retirement is deferred (i.e., the same effect as defined-contribution plans), the primary burden for earlier retirement will fall primarily on defined-benefit pension plans.

Postretirement Dissavings

The whole concept of postretirement dissavings is also worthy of consideration. We tend to look upon defined-benefit pension plans as life incomes, perhaps with survivor benefits included. If a significant portion of the private pension system is to be based upon capital accumulation plans (i.e., defined-contribution plans and personal Individual Retirement Accounts), consideration needs to be given as to how the capital accumulation resource should, or can, be used effectively to provide retirement income.

By way of a simplistic example, consider the alternatives which might be made available to the employee illustrated in Table 8–2, based upon retirement at age 65, with Social Security providing 25 percent of final pay and investment income of 8 percent per year:

1. If the individual were to convert the defined-contribution lump sum of $229,700 into a tax-free exchange for a life annuity, the percentage of preretirement pay replaced might be:

a.	Social Security	25%
b.	Defined-benefit pension	27
c.	Defined-contribution annuity	28
d.	Total	80%

2. On the other hand, suppose intermediate-term government bonds are yielding 10 percent at the time of retirement, a potentially interesting alternative might be available by rolling the lump-sum defined contribution into an IRA for six years prior to conversion to a life annuity:

		Age 65–70	*Age 71 and Over*
a.	Social Security	25%	25%
b.	Defined-benefit pension	27	27
c.	Defined-contribution annuity	0	59
d.	Total	52%	111%

Alternative (2) might be quite attractive if the individual intends to remain in the work force until the age IRA payments *must* commence.

The point of this exercise is to demonstrate the flexibility available from a combination program of Social Security, defined-benefit plan, and capital accumulation plan (including personal IRA accumulations). Thus, as existing supplemental defined-contribution plans and personal IRAs mature, considerable flexibility will automatically build itself into the system provided the concept of a pragmatic approach to the actual application of dissavings becomes better understood.

Health-Care Coverage

The role of health-care cost coverage in the retirement decision-making process will, I believe, become a major issue. The entire health-care delivery system is undergoing major change. The effect of this change on older people remains to be seen. It has been estimated that some 30 to 40 percent of the total health-care cost in the United States is expended in the last year of life. It would seem doubtful that changes in the health-care delivery system will alter the percentage expended in the last year of life.

Medicare has made two changes of interest. First, employer-provided health-care coverage has become the primary payor, rather than the secondary payor, for employees remaining in employment after age 65. Second, Medicare will now prepay premiums for health maintenance organizations up to certain limits. At the same time, Medicare remains under financial pressure, which may result in significantly higher Part B premiums and/or cutbacks in overall coverage.

A front-page article in the *New York Times* of September 9, 1985, quotes Joseph A. Califano, Jr. former Secretary of Health, Education and Welfare, as stating that obligations of the private sector for postretirement health-care is close to $2 trillion for the 500 largest industrial companies alone, and that "it is one of the world's greatest time bombs." While the magnitude of the obligation may be questioned, the conclusion is 100 percent correct.

The current federal tax situation is considered most favorable for employer payments for health care. Such payments are fully deductible by the employer, and tax free with respect to the individual for whom the payments are made. On the other hand, the 1984 Deficit Reduction Act has placed severe restrictions on the ability of employers to prefund postemployment supplemental health-care costs by means of qualified tax-exempt trust funds. Thus, those employers who wish to expense postemployment health-care costs have limited access to external funding vehicles through the limited accumulation of reserves under either (1) group health-care contracts; and/or (2) tax-exempt trust funds established under Voluntary Employee Benefit Associations.

The only other repository would seem to be the accumulation of balance-sheet reserves on the corporate financial statements, offset to some extent by deferred tax credits. If, as expected, the Financial Accounting Standards Board ultimately requires expensing of postemployment health-care costs during active worklives, the accumulation of these balance-sheet reserves will become a major factor in the analysis of corporate financial statements.

Absent preretirement expensing, those corporations which provide postretirement health-care coverage have been, or soon will be, confronted with a rapid increase as the retired rolls become a larger and larger percentage of the active work force. Even those corporations which preexpense—but do not prefund—will be confronted with a rapid increase in cash expenditures as claims are actually paid.

From the employee's perspective, absent external prefunding, the postemployment supplemental health-care coverage is entirely contingent upon the continued economic health of the employer, which may or may not be of significant comfort. With the current federal deficit situation, it appears unlikely that Congress will soon allow tax incentives to encourage prefunding of postemployment supplemental health-care coverages.

If employers wish to plan strategically for the effective use of total retirement programs, significant attention must be given to the role, and security, of postretirement supplemental health-care coverage. For those retiring prior to age 65 and/or where the spouse is under age 65, the employer's postretirement health care coverage will be the only coverage until age 65.

Lack of an effective program of postretirement health care coverage may well become an influence in deferring the retirement decision. Employers may well want to consider developing a formal program under which an increase in matching contributions under the defined-contribution program—or at least identifying a portion of the existing match—is applied exclusively to provide for health-care coverage after retirement.

The decision of Medicare to provide prepayment of HMO premiums is leading to studies of how to price such premiums.[5] Cost analyses of this type may well make the development of formal programs related to applying capital accumulation plans to meet postretirement health-care costs a realistic consideration.

---

[5]See H. Dennis Tolley and Kenneth G. Manton, "Assessing Health Care Costs in the Elderly," *Transactions of the Society of Actuaries, 1984,* Vol. XXXVI.

Employee Contributions and Taxation

The signals from Washington are mixed as to the expected role of personal savings in the overall system.

The initiation of tax-deferred individual retirement accounts in 1974, along with subsequent liberalizations, sent a positive message. Further positive messages came in the form of tax-deferred salary reduction plans [Internal Revenue Code Section 401(k)] and tax-favored employee-spending accounts under so-called cafeteria welfare plans.

On the other hand, Social Security taxes remain tax disadvantaged. Thus, Social Security taxes require off-the-top payment (from after-tax income) of over 7 percent (higher for the self-employed) of gross earned income. Furthermore, the administration recently announced the elimination of Section 401(k) as part of its revised tax-simplification proposals.

Thus, the shifting of cost—and risk—from employers to employees in the areas of both retirement income and health-care protection for the aged remains under a cloud of indecision. Those who were looking toward tax incentives to encourage greater participation from personal savings may find this avenue closed for the time being until the federal deficit problem has been resolved. While perhaps understandable from a short-term political viewpoint, a significant potential financial resource for the future welfare of the aged appears to be endangered.

Role of Legislation

There can be no doubt that legislation, and the resulting regulatory process, has had a profound impact on private pensions over the past 20 to 25 years. Considering the legislative history in the private pension area, one is struck by the impression that it represents reaction to perceived ills in the system, or reaction to other social or economic issues which, in turn, affect the private pension system.

There is no indication that the Congress of the United States is the arena in which solutions can be designed to meet the future needs of the system. Indeed, Congress appears stymied in its ability to correct flaws in existing legislation, as witnessed by its inability to enact effective corrective legislation with respect to Title IV of ERISA.

The private-sector market forces will determine the future direction of the pension system, just as the private sector is taking the leading role in shifting the entire health-care delivery system. The private sector cannot, should not, and will not wait for the reactive, and often stifling, legislative and regulatory process.

Other Players

Other than the legislative and regulatory processes, many other players will perform significant roles in the future direction of the overall system. Thirty years ago, the leading players were generally restricted to insurance companies and their agents, trust departments of major banks, and consulting actuaries. Indeed, the legal profession was having difficulty finding a major role to play, and was concerned that consultants were engaged in unlawful practice.

This has obviously changed dramatically in the past 10 years. With ERISA, and the companion tax and social legislation, the legal profession has become a major player, no longer concerned with the possible competition from nonlegal consultants. With continued legislative and regulatory activity, along with accelerating litigation, the future role of the legal profession in the evolution of the system appears to be eminently secure.

Similarly, the explosion of invested assets has led to an equally preeminent role for money managers of all types. The insurance industry has risen from the ashes of deferred-annuity contracts to become a major force in the financial community serving the private pension industry by providing unique investment opportunities for guaranteed investment contracts of many types. So long as such contracts provide relatively high real rates of return, with the carrier supplying a risk buffer, this place seems secure. Additional opportunities will arise for the insurance industry to develop interesting combinations of guaranteed investment returns along with pooled mortality as more and more individuals move into the period during which they will draw down their savings and the proceeds from defined-contribution plans.

Other money managers of all persuasions—bonds, stocks, venture capital, mortgages, real estate, foreign investments, and so forth—have proliferated. There seem to be unlimited opportunities—with great financial rewards for the most successful—associated with both defined-benefit plans and defined-contribution plans.

Within the overall area of investment performance, quality evaluation will also need to be developed. Investment policy decisions are an integral part of the overall system, and evaluation techniques to measure performance while in compliance with such policies are essential. Compliance with established policy does not necessarily provide the greatest return in a given measurement cycle. Furthermore, investment policies must be constantly reviewed to comply with both market opportunities and the expected cash-flow requirements of the program.

As assets of defined-contribution plans grow, mature, and become an important ingredient in the payout stage, financial planners may well find a ready market for their services in helping individuals plan for the distribution of funds to accommodate their entire period of retirement. This activity will be quite different from the current activity of helping individuals deal with the savings and tax-deferral phase of their lives.

Designing programs to accomplish desired results while complying with legislation and regulation, along with the establishment of appropriate funding and investment policies, will undoubtedly remain the primary thrust of consulting firms. No other profession has, as yet, demonstrated an ability superior to consulting actuaries in establishing integrated policies with respect to plan design, funding, and investments. The basic technical training, experience, and continuing education opportunities within the actuarial profession appear likely to maintain this leadership role, given whatever directions or counterdirections occur as private pension programs continue to evolve.

Administrative and computer services will also thrive, but only for those who demonstrate superior quality. There is no room for error when dealing with the future financial support of millions of individuals. Employers are beginning to realize that quality is more important than price. Computer technology will allow integration of quality administrative computer services from a variety of sources. As a result, it appears likely that specialized computer services will develop from many directions with severe competition developing and controlling the ultimate cost.

One of the weakest areas appears to be that of communication with both employees and retirees. The legal and design complexities of the system make effective communications extremely difficult. Those who can communicate seem to have difficulty understanding the complexities, while those who understand the complexities have difficulty communicating. If these programs are to be effective, individuals must comprehend their provisions and be able to relate the provisions to their individual circumstances. I would suggest that the academic community could perform a most valuable service by developing a combination of skills in both analysis and communications. The skills required are significantly greater than those currently applied to prepare summary plan descriptions in the so-called understandable language of ERISA, and to produce employee benefit statements.

Within the broad area of analysis and communication, there is a current trend toward the development of preretirement group seminars. These seminars can be worthwhile and unrealistic at the same time. The combined financial, tax, economic, social, and communicative skills required are rare indeed. Also, with the exception of executive counseling services, employers are most reluctant to become involved in individual counseling.

The broad area of the impact of pension plans on corporate finance provides an additional area of required expertise, both from the perspective of corporate finance officers and financial analysts. As we witness the difficulties of the Financial Accounting Standards Board in attempting to develop policies with respect to more uniform expensing, measurement of pension obligations, and more meaningful disclosure, it becomes obvious that there are no easy answers. Combine these complexities with the issue of employee security versus asset reversion and/or balance-sheet reserves, and the issues involved become even clearer, while the answers do not. Given the heavy agenda already faced by the university business schools, perhaps it is too much to expect significant attention to be given to the financial and human-resource issues of the private pension system. On the other hand, the present level of understanding with respect to financial obligations, funding policies, and investment policies appears to be grossly inadequate.

The entire area of strategic planning cries out for the development of personnel and processes by which financial, social, and human-resource expertise can be directed toward the major issues related to the aged which will confront the system within the next quarter century and beyond. While these issues are the primary focus of this chapter, suffice it to say that the essential training ground does not appear to exist, other than on-the-job training within the system itself. Here again, institutions of higher learning might well perform a valuable future service to the successful evolution of the system.

Some of these functions will be carried out internally by employees with outside expertise called in as needed. Many employers, however, will be hard pressed to provide more than basic administration internally.

Whether internal or external, however, all employers, and everyone else involved in the system, should at least be aware of the forces at work. The key area of strategic planning, however, would seem to require particular involvement by those with an intimate knowledge of the plan sponsor, thus requiring significant internal involvement.

To summarize, private-sector retirement programs represent a major factor in the existing market-oriented social/economic system of the United States. It cannot be denied that they represent major allocations of savings and, as a result, are subjected to major social, economic, and tax pressures. However the system has adapted, perhaps even better than anyone might have expected 30 years ago given the outside pressures of the past 30 years. Thus, I am confident the system will continue to adapt in the future, and that defined-benefit plans will continue to play a significant role. Defined-benefit plans are, in fact, more adaptable in achieving strategically planned replacement ratios at predetermined retirement ages.

Someone suggested that the best tax reform act to legislate in 1985 would be to guarantee no change for 20 years. The same might be said of pension legislation, although neither is a realistic expectation. Millions of hours have been spent by highly qualified practitioners adjusting the private pension system to comply with legislation and regulation since ERISA was first enacted in 1974. Hopefully the pace of legislation and regulation might slow down so that some of this talent could be expended toward adapting the system to accommodate the demographic and economic pressures to come in the next 25 years.

The conclusion reached in my June 1983 article in the *Financial Executive* magazine remains appropriate today:

> The private sector simply must step to the forefront of retirement and other employee benefit issues. To this end, five guiding principles have emerged through the preceding pages. In summary form, they are as follows:
>
> - Keep risk-sharing issues clearly in focus.
> - Take a strategic view of the emerging work force.
> - Understand the psychological and emotional issues.
> - Develop preemptive solutions to emerging problems.
> - Offer employees real incentives to share in building financial retirement security.
>
> In order to manage the work force of the next century, we must help shape its identity and anticipate its needs. The real question is not whether the private sector can afford to take such an activist stance, but whether it can afford *not* to do so.

If we are not successful, the aged population may well be expected to exercise its position as the major political force in the United States by the end of the first quarter of the 21st century.

Tax Policy and Retirement Income: A Rational Model for the 21st Century

9

by Daniel I. Halperin*

Government has a pervasive influence on the delivery of postretirement income. Not only is Social Security[1] the backbone of this nation's retirement income system,[2] but private pension and savings plans, voluntarily established by employers, are required to meet certain minimal standards as to employees' eligibility to participate and their security of earned benefits.[3] In addition, earnings from certain employer-sponsored retirement income programs (so-called qualified plans)[4] and personal savings plans (IRAs)[5] are free of tax, enabling savings in the

---

*Professor of Law, Georgetown University Law Center, Deputy Assistant Secretary of Treasury for Tax Policy, 1978–80.

[1] Social Security Act of 1935, 42 U.S.C. Sections 301–1397(f), (1982).

[2] President's Commission on Pension Policy, *Coming of Age: Toward a National Retirement Income Policy* 11–12 (February 26, 1981) [hereinafter cited as *Coming of Age*]. For a brief history of the Social Security program, see Office of the Actuary, Social Security Administration, U.S. Department of Health and Human Services, *History of the Provisions of Old-Age, Survivors, Disability, and Health Insurance 1935–1981*, Pub. No. 11–11515 (January 1982).

[3] Employee Retirement Income Security Act of 1974 (ERISA), 29 U.S.C. Sections 1001 et seq. See also Allen, "Trends Resulting From the Current Tax Treatment of Employee Benefits"; in *Why Tax Employee Benefits?* ed. D. Salisbury (1984), p. 25.

[4] IRC Sections 401, 410–417.

[5] IRC Section 408.

favored form to build at a pre-tax rather than an after-tax rate of return.[6]

The special tax treatment seems designed to channel saving for retirement but the applicable rules are not totally consistent with that aim. Below I suggest stricter adherence to the retirement goal. More flexibility, however, suits those who favor an incentive for savings in any form. They may believe an incentive is needed to overcome a bias against savings caused by taxing income rather than consumption.[7] Since there is no consensus in favor of a consumption tax, it is, perhaps, understandable that supporters of such a change would seek indirect means of accomplishing their goal. Expanding the special treatment for pension and profit-sharing plans into what looks more like a general incentive for saving is one such route. Some say Congress had this intention when it approved so-called section 401(k) plans in 1978 and expanded the availability of IRAs in 1981.[8]

It is not clear, however, that a reduction in the tax burden on investment income would substantially increase the rate of savings, and even some who favor a consumption tax over an income tax do not justify the change on this basis. They argue that increased savings could be achieved more efficiently by other means, such as a reduction of the deficit.[9] It would seem clear, in any event, that a savings incentive would be more cost effective if it operated on the margin rather than being subject

---

[6] In addition, the employer is allowed a current deduction for contributions it makes to qualified plans even though the employee's tax is deferred [IRC Sections 402(a), (404)(a)(1)(2)(3)]. The deduction for an IRA contribution by an individual is comparable (IRC Section 219). While this temporarily increases the assets in private hands, it does not reduce the tax burden in *present value terms* unless, as often occurs, the individual's marginal tax rate is reduced after retirement. The advantage of a reduced rate after retirement can also be achieved by use of a nonqualified plan. See Halperin, "Interest in Disquise: Taxing the 'Time Value of Money,' " *Yale Law Journal* 95 (January 1986), pp. 506, 539–40.

[7] A consumption tax differs from an income tax precisely in that the former allows an immediate deduction for all forms of savings. See generally Andrews, "A Consumption-Type or Cash Flow Personal Income Tax," *Harvard Law Review* 87 (1974), p. 1113.

[8] Prior to 1981, individuals who participated in employer plans could not also contribute to IRAs.

[9] See Aarron and Galper, *Assessing Tax Reform* 40 (Washington, D.C.: Brookings Institution, 1985).

to the limits that would inevitably govern a program with a retirement flavor.

It seems to me, therefore, that the debate over the desirability of more favorable treatment for investment income as opposed to income from labor should be separated from the question of the government's role in providing for retirement income. Under this view, the special treatment of retirement savings must rest on a distinction between savings for retirement and savings for other purposes.

There appears to be an assumption that it is extraordinarily difficult to plan for retirement on one's own. Whether because of the long time horizon, the press of more immediate needs, or the uncertainty of mortality, many people cannot or will not provide for their own retirement security.[10] Social Security provides for those unable to afford the high costs of individual annuities[11] as well as those too uninformed or myopic to prepare in advance for their retirement.[12]

Social Security payments, however, are insufficient to replace preretirement earnings, except perhaps for relatively low-wage, one-worker families.[13] Hence, unless Social Security

---

[10]Feldstein, "Social Security," in *The Crisis in Social Security*, ed. M. Boskin, (1977) pp. 17–18. See also Ross, "Why Social Security?" in *Readings in Social Security*, ed. W. Haber and W. Cohen (1948), p. 4; and Thompson, "The Social Security Reform Debate," 21 *Journal of Economic Literature* 1425 (1983), pp. 1440–42.

[11]Feldstein, "Social Security," p. 19.

[12]Ibid., pp. 20–21.

[13]The replacement rate is a measure of the sufficiency of replacement by Social Security benefits of the worker's preretirement income. Because of the sharply progressive Social Security benefit formula and the statutory minimum benefit, there is a great disparity among the replacement rates for low- and upper-income benefit recipients. For example, a single earner who retired at age 65 in 1983 after a full career of Social Security coverage would have had replaced 63 percent of his preretirement income if he had worked full time at the mimimum wage, 46 percent of his preretirement income if he had worked full time at the "average" wage ($14,400 per year), or 26 percent of his preretirement income if he had worked full time at the maximum taxable (for Social Security purposes) wage ($32,400 per year in 1983).

Because of the 1977 amendments to the Social Security laws, replacement rates will drop in the future, with the rate for the "average" worker slated to be as low as 39 percent by 1990. (Hays/Huggins Co. Inc., *Social Security* (1983), p. 18.) Most corporate plans define an "adequate" replacement rate as ranging from 70 to 80 percent of preretirement income for lower-paid employees. Subcommittee on Civil Service, Post Office, and General Services of the Senate Committee on Governmental Affairs, 98th Cong., 2d Sess., *Forums on Federal Pensions Part 5—Program Options* 21 (Comm. Print 1984). (Statement of Harper L. Garrett, Jr.) See also *Coming of Age*, p. 15.

benefits increase, the government's interest in the provision of adequate retirement income, even for low and moderate earners, necessarily extends to private savings.

A concern for particular individuals rather than the total level of savings suggests that a limit on the amount of the tax-favored accumulation would be appropriate. The precise amount, of course, cannot be scientifically determined. I would not restrict the target group to those who earn below the Social Security limit. Quite clearly, many who earn in excess of the wages covered by Social Security, now $39,600, cannot easily save for retirement.

On the other hand, a qualified plan presently can provide a defined benefit of as much as $90,000 per year.[14] Depending upon the intended relation between the pension and preretirement earnings, this suggests a focus on replacement of between $120,000 (75 percent replacement) and $150,000 of wages (60 percent replacement). The defined-contribution limit of the lesser of $30,000 or 25 percent of pay requires that $120,000 be earned before the maximum can be contributed.[15] Moreover, an annual contribution of $30,000 could very easily produce a benefit well in excess of $90,000 per year. Participation in several plans could further increase the total accumulation.

Present law permits tax-favored savings well in excess of the level for which government assistance can be justified.[16] It seems to me that the aim more properly should be adequate replacement of wages up to approximately twice the level covered by Social Security. Accordingly, this chapter will examine how tax incentives could be structured so as to more completely bridge the gap between Social Security and the in-

---

[14]IRC Section 415(b).

[15]IRC Section 415(c).

[16]President Reagan recommends making the intended present limit on tax-favored savings a reality by imposing a special excise tax on annual distributions from all tax-favored arrangements, including defined-contribution plans or IRAs, in excess of a specified amount. *The President's Tax Proposals to the Congress for Fairness, Growth, and Simplicity*, chap. 14.02 (May 1985). [Hereinafter cited as *The President's Tax Proposals.*] I believe this approach has the promise of substantial simplification if it is in fact possible to relate the excise tax to the benefit of the tax-free buildup. But, as suggested in the text, I would aim for a lower level of tax-favored accumulation. If the present approach is maintained, I would favor reducing the defined contribution limit to substantially less than one third of the defined-benefit limit.

come level necessary to maintain a preretirement standard of living for the low- and moderate-wage earner.

I do not write on a clean slate. The administration and Congress began an extensive examination of private retirement programs more than 20 years ago under President Kennedy.[17] This study culminated in 1974 with passage of the Employee Retirement Income Security Act (ERISA).[18] Since then, Congress has continued to enact piecemeal legislation on the subject[19] and President Reagan has proposed additional modifications.[20] There also have been several suggestions for more fundamental change,[21] including those of a Presidential Commission on Retirement Income appointed by President Carter.[22]

Despite all this attention, we are still groping for a more perfect solution. There are a number of reasons why this is so. One is certainly the difficulty inherent in using tax incentives to encourage the provision of retirement income for low and moderate earners upon whom the tax savings have little impact. Tax exemption of earnings favors the higher-income person who is most likely to be able to save on his own.[23]

---

[17]President Kennedy established the cabinet-level Committee on Corporate Pension Funds and Other Private Retirement and Welfare Programs on March 28, 1962. For a discussion of this Committee and governmental efforts to improve private income plans in the pre-ERISA years, see Senate Special Committee on Aging, 98th Cong., 2d Sess., *The Employee Retirement Income Security Act of 1974: The First Decade*, chap. 1 (Comm. Print 1984). [Hereinafter cited as *The First Decade*.]

[18]For one view of ERISA and a more detailed treatment of some of the issues discussed in this paper, see Halperin, *Retirement Security and Tax Equity: An Evaluation of ERISA, B.C.L. Review* 17 (1976), p. 739. See also Tax Notes 10 (1980), p. 803. (Interview of D. Halperin on Pension Issues.)

[19]See D. Salisbury, ed., *Why Tax Employee Benefits?*, p. 99. (A listing of legislation); Retirement Equity Act of 1984 (REA), Pub. L. No. 98–397. For brief but thorough explanations of the retirement-income-related provisions of the post-ERISA legislation, see *The First Decade*, chap. 3. For an explanation of the Retirement Equity Act of 1984 (REA), see Terry and Smith. *Guide to Retirement Equity Act of 1984*, Tax Notes 24 (1984), p. 1196.

[20]*The President's Tax Proposals*, chap. 14.

[21]E.g., H.R. 4330, 97th Cong., 1st Sess. 127 Cong. Rec.188194 (July 30, 1981), (Erlenborn bill). On October 22, Representative Clay and Senator Heinz introduced the Retirement Income Policy Act of 1985.

[22]*Coming of Age*, pp. 11–12.

[23]Since tax exemptions allow all individuals to accumulate earnings at a pretax rate of return, some view the tax treatment as equal. See Andrews, *Consumption-Type or Cash Flow*, pp. 1117–18, 1167–69. Nevertheless, this "equality" is inconsistent with the progressive income tax.

The nondiscriminaton test attempts to ameliorate this difficulty in employer-sponsored pension programs. Favorable tax treatment is generally limited to plans that do not discriminate (in the relationship of benefits or contributions to compensation) in favor of the so-called prohibited group of owners, officers, and other highly paid employees.[24] If this high-income group desires to take advantage of the tax benefits, they must assure actual participation by low-wage employees. The goal of tax policy may be to strengthen this standard.

But there is tension in any attempt to make the nondiscrimination test more stringent. As we seek to mold private voluntary arrangements so as to more closely conform with the requirements of public policy, we may move too far from the goals of the private parties, thereby causing these arrangements to terminate.[25] Thus, under the current scheme of incentives, there is always a choice—fewer but better plans, or less satisfactory arrangements in greater number.

To summarize, it must be the extraordinary difficulty of saving for retirement that justifies government aid in the form of the Social Security program and the tax incentives for private savings. Tax incentives are ineffective if directed (as is the case with IRAs)[26] solely at the individual. They are appropriate, if at all, only for employer-sponsored plans which *actually* provide significant retirement income for low- and moderate-income employees.

This chapter first will consider why particular employees may not be entitled to receive benefits when they retire even though the company they work for has a plan in force. Next, I turn to employees who are entitled to retirement benefits but may not receive enough to replace preretirement income. This may be so even though the employer's plan is intended to provide adequate retirement income for full-career employees and

---

[24]IRC Section 401(a)(4)(5), 411(d)(1).

[25]See, e.g., Special Committee on Aging, 98th Cong., 2d Sess., *10th Anniversary of the Employee Retirement Income Security Act of 1974: A Report of Conference Proceedings* 47 (Comm. Print 1984). (Statement of Walter Holan, president of Profit Sharing Council of America, hereinafter cited as *ERISA 10th Anniversary Conference Proceedings*.)

[26]IRAs could be more directed to those with lower income by phasing out the deduction for contributions as income rises or changing from a deduction to a credit for amounts contributed.

the individual is employed for his entire working life by such an employer. Finally, I consider whether the mechanism of voluntary employer plans, particularly if modified as suggested in the first two sections, can be expected to produce adequate coverage and, if not, whether alternative approaches to retirement security are viable.

Coverage

The nondiscrimination test does not assure benefits for low- and moderate-income employees. Participating employees may not stay on the job long enough to earn vested benefits, or if they do, they may withdraw the funds provided for them before retirement. Employees may be denied coverage because of their job classification or because they fail to contribute to contributory or salary-reduction plans. I believe the most important technique for restricting coverage is "integration," which permits the benefits employees receive from Social Security to be considered as part of the plan. I consider below possible ways to increase the proportion of benefits from qualified plans inuring to low and moderate earners.

Participation

Under present law, a plan will not qualify for tax-favored status if it discriminates in participation in favor of the "prohibited group"—employees who are officers, shareholders, or highly compensated.[27] The Treasury regulations, however, allow a "reasonable difference" between the ratio of the participating prohibited-group members, and the similar ratio of participating nonmembers of the prohibited group.[28]

[27]IRC Section 410(b) (1) (B). There is also a mechanical test allowed by the Code—70 percent of employees who have satisfied the conditions as to age and service are benefited, or 80 percent of all employees eligible to benefit under the plan are benefited if at least 70 percent of all employees are eligible to participate in the plan, exclusive of those precluded from eligibility for failure to meet age and service requirements. IRC Section 410(b) (1) (A). Some would argue in favor of a different mechanical test. Note "Discrimination in the Coverage of Retirement Plans," *Yale Law Journal* 90 (1981) pp. 817, 825–26.

[28]Treas. Reg. Section 1.410(b)-1(d) (2).

There is neither a clear definition of the prohibited group or a specific cutoff point at which the disparity between these ratios becomes unreasonable. For example, a plan in which 14.1 percent of the nonprohibited group members participated was considered qualified while another plan in which 11.1 percent of this group participated was deemed discriminatory.[29] One hundred percent of the prohibited group members participated in both plans. The difference in result appears to turn on the presence of factors other than the minimal difference in the ratios of nonprohibited group participation.

Recent rulings indicate that relevant factors in determining whether a coverage classification is discriminatory are the proportion of the total work force covered, the number of employees in *all* compensation ranges covered, whether the compensation of those covered is essentially the same as those not covered, and whether employees with low or moderate incomes are covered in more than nominal amounts.[30] These factors indicate that if the plan provides for a significant *number* of lower-paid people, there will be less concern that it may cover a larger *proportion* of the higher paid. Such a plan has at least accomplished something for which government aid is appropriate. The more difficult and unanswered question is the required relationship between the amount of such aid and the benefit obtained by the higher income.

President Reagan seeks both greater certainty and wider coverage among the lower paid by defining the prohibited group and permitting coverage of its members to exceed the proportion of coverage among nonmembers by only 25 percent.[31] An objective standard has obvious advantages but it appears unlikely that one can be devised which would be sufficiently flexible to respond to perceived differences in circumstances

---

[29]Rev. Rul. 83-58, 1983-1 C.B. 95; Rev. Rul. 83-94, 1983-2 C.B. 75, respectively.

[30]Rev. Rul. 83-58, Rev. Rul. 84-150, 1984-2 C.B. 99.

[31]*The President's Tax Proposals*, chap. 14.09. The prohibited group would include any person who at any time during a three-year period ending on the last day of the plan year was an owner of 1 percent or greater of the employer, an employee whose annual compensation equaled or exceeded $50,000, an employee whose annual compensation was greater than $20,000 and who was in the top 10 percent of employees by compensation, or an employee who was a family member of a prohibited group member. (The compensation and percentage figures would be adjusted for inordinately large or small employers.)

without also opening up opportunities for abuse.[32] For example, a broad definition of the prohibited group will permit a showing of nondiscrimination, despite disparate participation at the very highest levels, merely because the lower-paid members of the prohibited group are not covered by the plan. On the other hand, if the prohibited group is narrowly defined, a plan limited to those just below the cutoff would be acceptable even though this group is relatively high paid. In these circumstances, employers may prefer nonqualified plans for the very highest paid if exclusion of relatively few employees provides total flexibility as to participation in the qualified plan.

A more promising route may be to focus on the reasons which now permit an employer to cover less than 100 percent of the work force and to determine which of these may be acceptable. The published rulings involve plans which are limited to salaried and clerical employees and exclude hourly paid workers.[33] The Code now provides that such a classification is not per se discriminatory.[34] It is not clear why this should be. Hourly paid workers as a group seem as much in need of retirement protection as salaried workers.[35] There is no apparent reason why an employer with a large number of low-paid clerical workers should be allowed to limit its plan to salaried workers while an employer with fewer clerks cannot. If this approach makes sense, would employers with even larger numbers of clerks be allowed to exclude some of them?

---

[32]See. e.g., *Hearings on Retirement Income Security in the United States Before the Subcommittee on Oversight of the House Committee on Ways and Means* [hereinafter cited as *1985 Hearings on Retirement Income Security*], statement of American Society of Pension Actuaries, September 5, 1985 (elements of proposed definition of prohibited group discriminate against small business); statement of Joseph J. Martingale, Benefits Development Manager of J.C. Penney Co., Inc., September 6, 1985 (some of America's most broadly available and least discriminatory retirement plans would be deemed discriminatory); statement of the Chamber of Commerce of the United States, September 6, 1985 (strict, uniform proposed coverage rules do not allow enough flexibility, could cause companies with 100 percent coverage to lose tax-qualified status); statement of James D. Short, member of Board of Directors, The ERISA Industry Committee, September 5, 1985 (proposed mechanical coverage tests could disqualify companies with 100 percent worker coverage).

[33]Rev. Rul. 83-58; supra n. 29; Rev. Rul. 83-94; supra n. 29; Rev. Rul. 84-150; supra n. 30.

[34]IRC Section 401 (a) (5). Treas. Reg. Section 1.401-3(d).

[35]Hourly paid workers subject to a collective bargaining agreement are not included in the application of the coverage rules. IRC Section 410 (b) (3) (A).

Less than 100 percent coverage in a plan also occurs when an employer has separate plans for different plants or divisions. This seems more justified, particularly when there is a history of separate ownership.[36] I recognize the difficulty of identifying truly separate operations, but it seems possible that administerable rules could be developed. Perhaps significant abuse can be mitigated by requiring top management to participate in the least generous plan.

Even 100 percent coverage would not necessarily indicate that the plan provides significant aid to low and moderate earners. For example, a highly paid consultant may have no employees. Therefore, a limit on the proportion of benefits that may be provided to business owners[37] or other highly paid individuals should be considered. Similar restrictions now apply to other tax-favored fringe benefits[38] and President Reagan would expand their coverage.[39] If such a rule were in place, there may be less reason to be concerned about short-lived plans established when the principal owner is close to retirement.[40]

Integration with Social Security

To obtain favorable tax treatment, it is not necessary for the employer plan to treat the low and high paid equally. The plan may provide greater proportionate benefits for the higher paid

---

[36]See *1985 Hearings on Retirement Income Security*, statement of the Chamber of Commerce of the United States, September 6, 1985 (proposed coverage rules would produce particularly anomalous results for companies in multiple lines of business, where industry practices provide for different types and levels of employee benefits).

[37]A plan which does not provide significantly for nonowners is in effect an Individual Retirement Account and does not deserve the more favorable treatment reserved for qualified plans.

[38]See IRC Sections 120 (c) (3) (group legal service); 125 (b) (2) (cafeteria plans—applicable to key employees); 127 (b) (3) (educational assistance); 129 (d) (4) (dependent care).

[39]*The President's Tax Proposals*, chap. 3.04.

[40]Under present law, an individual must have 10 years of service with the employer to be entitled to the maximum $90,000 benefit. Changing the test to 10 years of participation would properly encourage earlier adoption of the plan. See *The President's Tax Proposals*, chap. 14.04. There is, of course, an advantage to establishing the plan when an employee is young, as this maximizes the accumulation of tax-free savings. The choice could be more readily left to the owner if the proportion of contributions that could inure to his benefit were limited to 25 percent or less.

as long as the combined effect of the plan and Social Security is nondiscriminatory. Social Security provides benefits based on a limited level of wages—$39,600 in 1985.[41] It is thus argued that the role of private pension plans is to provide benefits based on earnings above this limit.[42] A private pension plan need not benefit workers earning below $39,600 *unless* the level of replacement it provides above this point exceeds the value of Social Security with respect to the earnings to which it relates.[43]

This explanation for "integration" cannot be justified. I believe the special tax treatment for nondiscriminatory private plans exists precisely because Social Security does not adequately replace preretirement income even for low- and moderate-income workers. To give tax benefits to plans that provide little or nothing for these workers perverts this purpose.

This does not mean that Social Security should be ignored in determining the level of pension benefits. Since Social Security provides a higher level of replacement for the low-income worker,[44] a private plan with a goal of full wage replacement[45] will need to provide proportionately greater benefits for those with higher wages if it is not to provide more than is necessary to replace preretirement earnings for the lower paid. There is no reason to force savings to the point that some employees will have more income after retirement than they had available

[41]Joint Committee on Taxation, *Overview of Tax-Favored Retirement Arrangements* 16 (Comm. Print 1985).

[42]See, e.g., Allen, "Trends," pp. 30–31.

[43]IRC Section 401 (a) (5); 401 (l). For example, employer contributions of 5.7 percent only on earnings above $39,600 in 1985 are permissible. (5.7 percent is the scheduled required employer Social Security contribution rate through 1987.) *Overview of Tax-Favored Retirement Arrangements,* p. 16. See also Wolk, "Discrimination Rules for Qualified Retirement Plans: Good Intentions Confront Economic Reality," *Virginia Law Review* 70 (1984), pp. 419, 445–49.

[44]Allen, "Trends," p. 25.

[45]"Full wage replacement" will be somewhat less than 100 percent of preretirement earnings due to lower taxes and the elimination of expenditures associated with employment (e.g., transportation, clothing) and with raising children, as well as with mortgage payments. *Forums on Federal Pensions Part 5—Program Options,* p 21. (Statement of Harper L. Garrett.) Others point out that certain expenses increase at retirement, such as transportation costs associated with the particular needs and requirements of elderly people and health expenses not covered by Medicare (such as homemaker services). *Forums on Federal Pensions Part I—Economic Security Problems,* p. 21. (Statement of B. Seidman.)

while working.[46] Therefore, a plan which provides greater benefits in relation to pay for higher-income individuals could be deemed nondiscriminatory. It should be so considered, however, only if the plan together with Social Security provides full wage replacement for full-career employees and the combined benefit from the plan and Social Security does not favor the higher paid.

In short, the approach to integration must be modified to first assure "full replacement" for low- and moderate-income employees. Since Social Security alone will generally not fully replace preretirement earnings, a private plan will have to provide a "minimum" benefit for all low and moderate earners. The requirement of such a benefit under so-called top-heavy plans is thus on the right track[47] but the approach needs to be extended to all plans and adjusted so as to have a closer relationship to the amount needed for full replacement. President Carter's 1978 proposal would also prevent exclusion of employees merely because they do not earn above the level of wages covered by Social Security, but it would allow contributions above $39,600 to be approximately twice the level of contributions on earnings below that amount even if the plan does not attain full wage replacement.[48] Thus, it is only a second best

---

[46]Some would argue that there is little danger of this occurring as long as private plans do not adjust for inflation and coverage for a full career remains unlikely. These people would ban integration and test the private plan on its own. See, e.g., *Hearings on the President's 1978 Tax Reform Before the House Committee on Ways and Means*, 95th Cong., 2d Sess., 5576 (1978). (Statement of Karen Ferguson, Director, Pension Rights Center.)

[47]IRC section 416(c).

[48]Specifically, the Carter administration proposed that the percentage of benefits or contributions above the integration level (Social Security Maximum Taxable Wage Base) could not exceed 180 percent (later modified to 200 percent) of the benefits or contributions below the integration level. For defined-benefit plans employing the offset method, the percentage of pay provided as a benefit could not be offset by a percentage of PIA (Primary Insurance Amount) greater than the percentage benefit.

For example, under the Carter proposal an employer who in 1985 contributed 5.7 percent of pay on wages over $39,600 would be required to contribute at least 3.16 percent (2.85 percent under the modified proposal) of pay for employees earning under $39,600 annually. Likewise, an employer who provided a benefit of 65 percent of pay upon retirement could not offset that benefit by more than 65 percent of PIA, in contrast to the permissible offset of 83⅓ percent under the existing rules.

For a detailed explanation of the proposal and its effects on various types of plans, see *Hearings on National Pension Policies: Private Pension Plans Before the Subcommittee on Retirement Income and Employment of the House Select Committee on Aging*, 95th Cong., 2d Sess. (1978) pp. 234–50.

solution, justified by the prospect of substantial simplification of the rules for integration.[49]

Employee Option to Participate

With the limited exception for IRAs, special tax treatment is limited to "employer" contributions to employer-sponsored plans. Favorable tax results can be achieved, however, even if employees have a choice as to whether such contributions will be made. Under a contributory plan, an employee must be willing to make his or her own contributions in order to participate. These contributions may help finance a "defined-benefit" plan or under a so-called thrift plan may be "matched" by employer contributions at a specified ratio. Nonparticipants do not explicitly receive higher current wages.

Special rules adopted in 1978 (for so-called section 401(k) plans, also known as cash or deferred arrangements or CODAs) do allow tax deferral even though an employee, at her request, could receive current salary equal to the total amount that would otherwise be contributed to the plan.[50] These rules may permit "employee" contributions to thrift plans to be made on a tax-preferred basis.

The decision to participate in elective plans would presumably be governed by the availability of funds in light of the tax benefits for deferral.[51] Given the relative value of the tax savings, those who opt out of these arrangements are likely to come disproportionately from among those with low and moderate income. At first glance, therefore, plans which give the employee a choice between salary for current consumption and participation in a retirement program should not be enti-

---

[49]The present rules for integration are found in Rev. Rul. 71-446, 1971-2 C.B. 187. Many of the details would be unnecessary under the Carter proposal.

[50]The tax deferral allowed for Section 401(k) plans is contrary to the doctrine of constructive receipt which is ordinarily applied. Under this doctrine, if an employee has a choice to receive cash, he may be taxed even if the money is, at his direction, used for another purpose, such as deferred compensation. Treas. Reg. Section 1.451-2.

[51]Since the benefits to the employee are increased if the employer matches the employee contribution, such matching should increase participation. A 1983 survey of 246 companies with Section 401(k) plans showed that 83 percent of these companies matched employee contributions, at the average rate of 50 cents per dollar contributed by the employee. *ERISA 10th Anniversary Conference Proceedings*, p. 36. (Statement of Susan Koralik, partner, Hewitt Associates.)

tled to special tax treatment beyond that available under an IRA. Maximum impact from the nondiscrimination standard does not occur unless the employer requires participation.

While the current Treasury sometimes equates CODAs to IRAs, the 1978 Treasury did not object to the enactment of Section 401(k).[52] The principal reason for that decision may have been "history." Rules similar to Section 401(k) had been approved administratively by the IRS as early as 1956. It was also possible to approximate the effect of CODAs by indirect means, such as integration or early distributions to those who preferred not to participate. Thus it seemed impossible to change the approach, at least without grandfathering existing plans. The Treasury also recognized, however, the pressures for flexibility in the compensation package and the potential difficulty of distinguishing between employer and employee contributions. On balance, employee choice did not seem fatal if in fact nondiscriminatory participation was achieved. Such nondiscrimination as well as limited access to funds prior to retirement distinguishes Section 401(k) plans from IRAs.[53]

Some believe, moreover, that Section 401(k) increases overall coverage. They argue that since that contribution comes explicitly and directly out of wages, employers may be more willing to establish plans than if they had to count on being able to reduce pay or restrain wage increases to recoup their costs.[54] Thus, Section 401(k) would lead to retirement savings that would not otherwise exist.

A similar justification for contributory plans is possible, although more tenuous. The employer does not directly recoup his pension contributions through salary reduction. He does, however, have greater assurance that such contributions are only made on behalf of employees who value retirement benefits and thus will accept a lower level of current compensation. Although it may be difficult to selectively reduce salary of participants, the contributory requirement assures that the cost of

---

[52]Halperin, "Cash or Deferred Profit-Sharing Plans," *N.Y.U. Institute on Federal Taxation* 41 (1983), chap. 39, pp. 5–6.

[53]See, e.g., *ERISA 10th Anniversary Conference Proceedings*, p. 37. (Statement of Susan Koralik, partner, Hewitt Associates.)

[54]See *Hearings Before Senate Subcommittee on Labor*, October 1, 1985. (Statement of Karen Ferguson criticizing this claim.)

the plan will be minimized for the class of employees who do not value pensions and are least likely to accept a cut in pay. As discussed below, this will make the plan more desirable and more likely to be established.[55]

But employee choice cannot be justified merely by showing that the number of plans will be increased, even assuming it can be so proved. More plans are not necessarily desirable if the additional plans that are established are highly discriminatory. Moreover, there is an offsetting detriment to the extent that companies switch from nonelective plans to CODAs in which fewer employees participate.[56] This is particularly true if the former plan was a defined-benefit plan which offered greater assurance of adequate retirement income.

If the decline in coverage under existing plans or those that would be established in the absence of Section 401(k) outweighs the formation of plans that would not otherwise exist, it becomes more essential to reevaluate the strength of the factors that led to the original adoption of Section 401(k). This reexamination could indicate at least a need for a limit on maximum benefits from Section 401(k) plans in order to maintain the incentive for continuation or adoption of nonelective plans.[57] In any event, Section 401(k) plans must be made to satisfy the most stringent test for nondiscrimination. The discrimination now permitted in these plans must be prevented by changes, similar to those recommended by President Reagan, which would narrow the disparity between contributions for the highest paid and those for rank-and-file-employees.[58]

At present, CODAs must satisfy a mechanical test comparing the average contribution for the top-paid one third of eligible

---

[55]See Part III B *infra*.

[56]The recent growth in the popularity of salary-reduction plans may further erode the desire of employers to establish or improve tax-qualifed plans supported by employer contributions. *ERISA 10th Anniversary Conference Proceedings*, p. 13. (Statement of Thomas Woodruff, executive director, Commission on College Retirement). The likelihood of such switching was not adequately considered in 1978, perhaps because of the limited adoption of CODAs between the original IRS approval in 1956 and the change in policy in 1972, confirmed in 1974 by ERISA. Perhaps, even if the Code had been silent, a trend toward both defined contribution and flexibility would have heightened interest in the earlier ruling.

[57]See *The President's Tax Proposals*, chap. 14.06. (Recommending such a limit, apparently for other reasons.)

[58]Ibid.

employees to the average contribution for the remaining two thirds.[59] This approach raises three questions. First, does the one-third two-thirds division properly identify the "prohibited group" for whom more favorable treatment is forbidden? Second, should the comparison be based on averages or should the contribution for each member of the prohibited group be compared to the average contribution for nonmembers? Finally, should a disparity in the level of contributions for those eligible to participate be permitted in addition to the difference in eligibility, if any, which is generally allowed for all plans?

Since the top one third may include some relatively lower-paid employees who may choose not to participate, the current comparison may disguise much higher relative contributions for the *highest*-paid employees. For example, average contributions of 20 percent for those earnings in excess of $100,000 per year as compared to say 2 to 3 percent for the lowest-paid two thirds may be allowed merely because employees earning about $20,000 to $30,000 per year are in the top one third and do not participate significantly, thus sharply reducing the average contribution for the top one third. Narrowing the prohibited group would help, and limiting the group to the very highest paid would cure this particular difficulty. As indicated above, however, narrowing the group too much would permit disproportionate or even exclusive coverage for those dropped from the group who may still be relatively high paid.

Even if it were feasible to compare average contributions for narrow salary ranges, many would be uncomfortable with contributions on behalf of an individual earning $100,000 per year at a higher percentage than the average for the work force even if all individuals earning above $100,000, considered as a group, are not disproportionately favored. These people would compare the contribution for any one prohibited group member with the average contribution for nonmembers.

Uncomfortable is the word to use because it may be more a matter of feeling than logic. The rules for nonelective plans, which allow less than total coverage of the lower-paid employees whenever some higher paid are also excluded, suggest that the focus is on average participation. But in these plans partici-

[59] IRC Section 401(k)(4).

pants obtain comparable benefits; a higher-paid participant only receives more than lower-paid *nonparticipants*.

Under Section 401(k), one higher-paid participant can obtain higher benefits than some lower-paid eligibles. Is it troublesome that she may receive more than the *average* of the lower paid even if the average for all people in *her group* is comparable to the lower-paid average? I am not sure how I would answer that question. The answer depends upon a feel for the theory of the nondiscrimination test beyond what we have yet been able to articulate. Perhaps it would be best to test on an average basis for most members of the prohibited group while limiting the individual contribution for each employee above a specific *high*-compensation level.

In making this comparison of contribution levels either on an individual or group basis, the President's proposals recommend generally that the prohibited group be permitted a contribution level equal to 125 percent of the average contribution for nonmembers.[60] While less generous than present law, this proposed test will permit a higher level of contributions for the prohibited group than others. This is not allowed when there is no employee choice.[61]

However, Section 401(k) plans provide full and immediate vesting.[62] Despite equality in the initial contributions, nonelective plans effectively could provide more disproportionate benefits than Section 401(k) plans if greater than a 25 percent difference in the proportion of benefits that vest was tolerated. I know of no study of the difference in vesting which could occur without a plan being considered discriminatory in operation.

On the other hand, traditional contributory plans do not require immediate vesting. Therefore, if any tolerance in participation levels between the prohibited group members and all others is permitted on top of whatever difference in eligibility is allowed, contributory plans become even more discriminatory. Contributory plans also seem more unfair because a nonpar-

---

[60]*The President's Tax Proposals*, chap. 14.06.

[61]IRC Section 401(a)(4) provides that contributions or benefits provided under an employer plan cannot discriminate in favor of the prohibited class.

[62]IRC Section 401(k)(2)(C).

ticipating employee does not receive the employer contribution in cash. For this reason, the potential difficulty of distinguishing between employer and employee contributions, which is in some part responsible for the enactment of Section 401(k), does not arise.

On its face, the employer is "willing" to contribute part of the cost of the pension. Employees who fail to contribute could at least receive the "inadequate" benefit available from employer contributions. It is, of course, more likely that employees will contribute if access to employer contributions depends on willingness to do so[63] but the participation goal could be more readily reached by eliminating employee choice. Thus, I find traditional contributory plans more difficult to justify than CODAs. In any event, the *actual* level of participation in such plans should be required to meet the standard of noncontributory plans for "eligibility."

Vesting

Mere participation in a retirement plan is not enough to assure a benefit. The individual must satisfy conditions of vesting, which may require as much as 10 or even 15 years of service for full vesting. Since employees often change jobs after a shorter tenure, delayed vesting could seriously undermine the adequacy of benefits.[64]

Since ERISA, the code has required as a condition of qualification that a plan meet certain minimum standards for vesting of benefits.[65] Most plans choose no vesting for 10 years and full vesting thereafter.[66] In addition, faster vesting may be required if necessary to prevent discrimination in actual distribution of benefits to the prohibited group.[67] Controversy over the extent

---

[63]See *ERISA 10th Anniversary Conference*, p. 36.

[64]Senate Special Committee on Aging, *Developments in Aging: 1984*, 99th Cong., 1st Sess., Vol. 1 (1985), p. 50.

[65]IRC section 411(a)(2).

[66]Approximately 88 percent of the pension plans of medium and large companies have vesting (complete) after 10 years of service. *ERISA 10th Anniversary Conference Proceedings*, p. 56. (Statement of Edith Fierst.)

[67]IRC Section 411(d)(2).

of the IRS power to mandate faster-than-statutory vesting[68] has been mooted by the enactment of tougher vesting requirements for so-called top-heavy plans.[69]

Aside from the equity in more equal allocation of tax benefits between high- and low-paid or even short- and long-service employees, there is a "truth in pension" component to vesting. If his expectations are not met, an employee who prepares for retirement as if a benefit were forthcoming may be worse off than he would have been if no plan were established. On the other hand, if employees understood that benefits were uncertain and put aside additional amounts for retirement, they would unnecessarily reduce their current living standard if benefits in fact vest. In short, if it is appropriate and sensible for an employee to save for retirement at the point in his life when plan participation occurs, there may be no totally sensible way to react to benefits that are not fully vested. To take an oversimplified example, suppose it is appropriate to save $200 for retirement but the employee's pay is reduced by only $80, reflecting a 40 percent chance that he will earn a vested benefit. Additional savings of $120 would be inadequate in itself to provide for retirement and unnecessary if vesting occurs.

Employers may argue that delayed vesting rewards longevity and, thus, the most productive worker.[70] Even if turnover is to be discouraged, it seems better to reward longevity in the wage scale, given the difficulty delayed vesting imposes on an employee.

In sum, I believe that unless it can be shown that the existence of the plan neither affects the employee's wages or the adoption of a sensible private program for retirement savings, vesting should be required whenever a meaningful benefit is earned. Three points should be mentioned in this context.

First, the existence of a meaningful benefit for a young employee from a defined-benefit plan will depend upon whether the rules concerning calculation of such benefits can be modi-

---

[68]See Osgood, *Pension and Profit-Sharing Plan Vesting, Boston University Law Review* 59 (1979), pp. 452, 461.

[69]IRC Section 416(b).

[70]Munnell, *The Economics of Private Pensions* (1981), p. 21.

fied.[71] Second, the "cost" of increased vesting to an employer should depend upon whether additional contributions can be recouped by reduction of the salary of the newly vested employees.[72] It is worth considering whether the employee in the above example might be more willing to accept a $200 reduction in current pay in return for a fully vested benefit than he would be willing to accept an $80 reduction for what amounts to a lottery ticket with an objective 40 percent chance of success. Finally, faster vesting will not help ensure retirement security if benefits are distributed and spent upon separation from service. The possibility of preventing or at least discouraging such distributions is discussed in the next part.

Distributions Prior to Retirement

Taxable Distributions. Present law is not consistent with regard to preretirement distributions from tax-favored plans. Sometimes they are prohibited. In other situations distributions are discouraged by an excise tax. Finally, in some circumstances they are freely allowed and perhaps encouraged by favorable tax treatment. This part discusses possible modifications of the existing rules which would serve to preserve the benefits for retirement.

Pension plans are not entitled to tax exemption if they make distributions while employment continues.[73] They can pay benefits, in a lump sum if desired, upon separation from service or termination of the plan.[74] Profit-sharing plans other than Section 401(k) plans can make distributions while service continues although there may have to be a delay of two years between the contribution and the distribution.[75] Section 401(k) plans cannot pay benefits during employment unless the em-

---

[71] *Infra* Part II A.

[72] See *infra* Part III B. If the required vesting period for plans was reduced to five years, the increase in cost for most defined-benefit pension plans would range "from 0 to 7 percent of present plan costs and from 0 to 0.2 percent of compensation of covered employees." *The First Decade*, p. 131.

[73] Treas. Reg. Section 1.401-1(b)(1)(i).

[74] See Halperin, *Retirement Security*, p. 765.

[75] Treas. Reg. Section 1.401-1(b)(1)(ii); Rev. Rul. 71-295, 1971–2 C.B. 184.

ployee has reached age 59½ or has suffered a financial hardship.[76]

Distributions to 5 percent owners from a profit-sharing plan or from a pension plan on early separation from service or termination of the plan are subject to a special 10 percent excise tax unless the employee has reached age 59½.[77] A similar penalty applies to distributions from an IRA before such age.[78] Since the excise tax is imposed at a flat rate, it is much harsher in comparison to prior tax benefits on those who are subject to tax at a relatively low rate.

Ideally, annuity payments beginning at retirement or at a specified age, such as 70, would be the required form of distribution. This is consistent with the goal of providing income replacement in the postretirement years. Employers can avoid tracing former employees, particularly after early separation from service or termination of the plan, by the purchase of commercial annuities or perhaps by transferring the accumulated benefit to an IRA for the benefit of the employee.[79] If distributions from employer or individually established IRAs cannot be prohibited, at least they could be discouraged by a stiff excise tax.

Some would argue, however, that if in-service distributions from profit-sharing plans were prohibited or inhibited by a penalty, employees would be less willing to enter such arrangements.[80] In particular, it is claimed that further restrictions on withdrawals would cause participation in Section 401(k) and contributory plans to decline and would, in fact, reduce savings for retirement since in most circumstances preretirement distributions would not be made. If this is true, it is difficult to determine the right mix—free enough access to funds so as not to unduly discourage participation at the lower income levels, yet not so free that the prospect of providing retirement income is an illusion.

---

[76]IRC Section 401(k)(2)(B).

[77]IRC Section 72(m)(5).

[78]IRC Section 408(f).

[79]See *The First Decade*, pp. 132–33.

[80]Vine, "Cash or Deferred Arrangements: What's the Beef, What's at Stake?" *Virginia Tax Review* (Winter 1986, forthcoming).

To some extent, the issue is different and perhaps easier with respect to those with higher incomes. Such people can be expected to save on their own. In any event, the nondiscrimination test does not require that they participate. Therefore, the concern is not so much that those with higher income participate and leave the funds to retirement but that they be unable to take advantage of the tax benefits of an IRA or a qualified plan for short-term savings unrelated to retirement. This would require a greater penalty than the present 10 percent excise tax.[81] But at least in some sense, if the tax advantages are eliminated, early withdrawal is not a concern.

Such withdrawal by the low income, on the other hand, is inconsistent with the goal of the nondiscrimination test. This could justify a stiffer penalty. If the penalty is greater than the tax benefits, it would prevent the practice of contributions for the lower income followed by withdrawal as soon as feasible. Under present law, for example, an employee's accrued benefit under a "mandatory" profit-sharing plan need never exceed the value of the last two years' contributions.

On the other hand, as stated above, restrictions on withdrawal could preclude participation which might blossom into retirement income. In addition, a harsher penalty on the lower income would seem unfair if in fact early distributions do occur, particularly if the need for funds is unexpected and urgent.

This requires a difficult balancing. Low and moderate earners may have to be assured that if they need funds for unforeseen emergencies, they will at the least be no worse off than if they had not entered the plan in the first place.[82] This may make it essential to identify the purpose of a withdrawal despite the obvious difficulty of verifying individual personal circumstances. For example, distributions from profit-sharing plans could be allowed without penalty in the case of unforeseeable events such as medical emergencies or unemployment of a spouse and precluded because of mere passage of time.

I would prefer a total prohibition of withdrawals in other circumstances as well, particularly since I do not want to unnecessarily favor defined-contribution plans. If distributions must be allowed for such foreseeable events as purchase of a residence

---

[81]*ERISA 10th Anniversary Conference*, p. 37.

[82]Ibid.

or college tuition, the distribution should be subject to a penalty which, at the very least, would be sufficient to offset the benefit of the tax-free buildup. A similar penalty should apply to distributions from an IRA. An alternative or additional approach is to deny credit for preretirement distributions in testing for discrimination.

The administration seeks to reduce early withdrawals. It would subject all distributions prior to age 59½ to an excise tax and would increase the current 10 percent tax to 20 percent unless funds are used for college tuition, the purchase of a first residence, or the replacement of expired unemployment benefits.[83] As indicated, the competing considerations and multiplicity of circumstances make it difficult to devise an appropriate "penalty" for early withdrawal. If, as the administration states, the excise tax is intended to offset the benefit of the tax-free accumulation, it seems defective.

The tax advantage of a qualified plan can be described as the ability to earn a tax-free rate of return.[84] The extent of the advantage depends upon three factors: the actual rate of return, the marginal tax rate, and the length of time the funds are in the plan. It is obvious, therefore, that any formula which is not related to any of these factors must be completely arbitrary.

The lower the individual's marginal tax rate, the greater the penalty if it is unrelated to such a rate. As suggested above, a harsher penalty on the lower income is not necessarily illogical but it may not be acceptable in the case of true hardship. Perhaps a greater concern is that the penalty does not fully recapture the tax benefits of the highly paid. Thus, the excise tax will not prevent intentional use of an IRA or other vehicle for nonretirement savings. It does seem feasible to relate the penalty to the tax bracket at the time of withdrawal. The excise tax could be a percentage of the regular tax or the amount included in income could be increased by some multiple of the distribution.

It may also be possible to relate the penalty more closely to

---

[83] *The President's Tax Proposals*, chap. 14.02. This penalty would also apply to early distributions from an IRA. The administration also appropriately recommends the elimination of the special averaging rules for lump-sum distributions. Since tax can be deferred by a rollover to an IRA, the special averaging is an unwarranted benefit which only encourages early spending.

[84] *Infra*, Part III A.

the rate of return and the period of participation by basing the penalty (or the extra inclusion suggested above) on the excess of the distribution over the original contribution rather than the total distribution.

Loans. In certain circumstances, loans from qualified plans are permitted where distributions would be prohibited.[85] Moreover, loans that do not exceed specified statutory limits are not taxed to employees as distributions would be.[86]

For policy reasons, loans may be preferable to distributions because loans presumably will be repaid, thus making funds available for retirement. Otherwise, a loan is more troublesome. First, the tax benefit of the qualified plan (tax-free buildup within the plan) continues even though the funds ostensibly accumulated for retirement have been withdrawn from the plan. Second, a loan may create negative retirement income if the total of the obligation to the plan and the tax on the distribution exceeds the amount distributed at the time of retirement.

Under current law, loans are taxable unless required to be repaid within five years (or a longer reasonable time if in connection with a purchase or improvement of a principal residence).[87] The administration proposes to make the 5-year limit a reality by in effect prohibiting reborrowing for a 12-month period after repayment and by limiting the exception for residence loans to the first purchase of a residence.[88]

The administration recommendations are clearly appropriate. Moreover, if loans cannot be totally prohibited, a deduction for interest on loans to qualified plans should be denied.

Security of Benefits

An ideal plan would provide employees with a benefit package which, when combined with Social Security, would provide "full replacement" of preretirement income.[89] But plans de-

[85]See *The President's Tax Proposals*, chap. 14.08.

[86]IRC Section 72(p)(2).

[87]IRC Section 72(p)(2)(B).

[88]*The President's Tax Proposals*, chap. 14.08.

[89]See note 13.

signed to achieve this goal may not succeed even for an employee who has not forfeited any benefits and who has had a full career of service for an employer with such a plan.

A defined-benefit plan will not live up to the ideal of "full replacement" if the employee changes jobs, the plan does not provide for postretirement inflation, or the plan has insufficient assets upon termination and benefits are not fully insured by the PBGC.

A defined contribution plan, with the goal of full replacement, will prove inadequate if the plan earnings are lower or compensation rose faster than anticipated. It will also not provide a sufficient benefit for the employee who began service before the plan was adopted or who for some reason is required to retire early.

I believe that a defined-benefit plan is more likely to provide retirement security. I discuss in this section means of strengthening that promise and more importantly the possibility of mitigating both employer and employee resistance to defined-benefit plans. An additional possibility, not considered herein, is a restriction on defined-contribution plans.

Defined Benefit versus Defined Contribution

Nature of the Promise. A defined-benefit plan provides a specified benefit, ordinarily a percentage of pay for each year of service, including service prior to the establishment of the plan. The employee is not affected by investment performance and, if benefits are based on "final" pay rather than "career average," by unexpected changes in earnings due to inflation.[90] Once in pay status, however, benefits ordinarily do not automatically increase with changes in the cost of living, although most large employers have provided ad hoc increases.[91]

---

[90]*ERISA 10th Anniversary Conference*, p. 45. (Statement of Vance Anderson, employees' relations counsel, Mobil Oil Corp.) See also *Forums on Federal Pensions Part* 5, p. 7. (Statement of Clifford I. Gould, Assistant to the Comptroller General for Federal Retirement Matters, U.S. General Accounting Office, indicating that most plans are based on final pay.)

[91]*Forums on Federal Pensions*, p. 20. (Statement of Harper L. Garrett, Jr.) Garrett points out that even with the ad hoc increases, rarely if ever is the full impact of the cost of living recognized and adequately accounted for.

This type of plan still predominates.[92] However, some report an increasing trend toward so-called defined-contribution plans.[93] Under a defined-contribution plan, the employer makes a contribution, usually a percentage of pay. The benefit depends upon investment performance and the amount in the employee's account.

It would be unusual in these cases, even if the employer has a retirement income goal in mind, to communicate the aim to employees. Still, a defined-contribution plan could in theory be designed to produce a certain level of benefits equal to a proportion of final pay. Contributions would depend upon estimates of both investment performance and changes in pay over time.[94]

While defined-contribution plans do not ordinarily adjust contributions to reflect prior service,[95] it is possible to do so, particularly in a type of defined-contribution plan called a target-benefit plan. Assuming a certain level of plan earnings, the contribution to such a plan is intended to provide a specified percentage of salary per year of service. If contributions are adjusted to reflect changes in salary, these plans parallel defined-benefit plans except for investment risk.

Defined-contribution plans, with the possible exception of the few target-benefit plans, are not well designed to accomplish the purpose of assuring adequate retirement income. The employee does not have a clear idea of the relationship of his expected benefit to preretirement income. Even if a sensible goal is set by the employer, its achievement is affected by how closely investment performance and changes in compensaton conform to the employer's projection. Further, there is ordinarily no coverage for service prior to the establishment of the plan.

---

[92]Ibid., p. 28. Most larger employers use integrated defined-benefit plans to provide the basic benefit and use defined-contribution plans to provide supplementary benefits.

[93]*ERISA 10th Anniversary Conference*, pp. 48–49. (Statement of Lawrence Margel, vice president and chief actuary, Towers, Perrin, Forster, and Crosby Consultants.)

[94]Many point out that, at best, defined-contribution plans can target benefits only "on average." See, e.g., Ibid., p. 47 (statement of Lawrence Margel); p. 49, (statement of Vance Anderson); *Forums on Federal Pensions*, p. 26, (statement of Harper L. Garrett).

[95]At least one large corporation indicates that it has been unable to accomplish the objectives of recognizing past service and salary history when using defined-contribution plans. *ERISA 10th Anniversary Conference*, p. 44. (Statement of Vance Anderson.)

Nevertheless, there are a number of reasons why employers might prefer defined-contribution plans to defined-benefit plans. Further, although older employees would prefer defined-benefit plans or other arrangements which take account of past service, younger employees tend to prefer defined-contribution plans. The reasons for this bias on behalf of both employers and employees is described in the next two parts.

Employee Preference for Defined-Contribution Plans. Some reasons that employees prefer defined-contribution plans, such as easier access to funds prior to retirement, are not legitimate given the purpose of the special tax treatment. A more rational and consistent treatment of early distributions would eliminate this preference or at least substantially reduce it. Other benefits from defined-contribution plans, such as the likelihood of faster vesting, are more a matter of custom than dependent upon the nature of the plan.[96] Again, faster required vesting for all plans could eliminate this advantage. If plan earnings reflect a real rate of return on top of the rate of inflation, defined-contribution plans do present the possibility of automatically adjusting for inflation even after retirement. We should consider the possibility of precluding defined-benefit plans from reducing real (inflation-adjusted) benefits, just as they now cannot reduce nominal benefits, at least in those circumstances where the investment return under the plan increases by the rate of inflation.

The most significant reason why defined-contribution arrangements are more beneficial for younger employees is the measurement of vested benefits. For example, assume an employee terminates employment at age 35 after 10 years of participation in a defined-benefit plan. If the benefit is 1 percent per year of service, he would have earned a 10 percent benefit based on compensation at time of termination. This does not take account of expected future increases in real earnings, or even nominal salary changes due to inflation.

In contrast, if the contribution level of a defined-benefit plan anticipates a certain level of benefits based on estimated final

---

[96] *ERISA 10th Anniversary Conference*, p. 40. (Statement of S. Koralik.)

pay, the percentage of contributions and hence the accumulation will be greater than if no increase in pay were anticipated. Further, benefits would increase with inflation to the extent inflation is reflected in investment performance.

It would be possible to require defined-benefit plans to provide terminated employees with a benefit more closely related to final pay. If distribution is deferred until the employee reaches retirement, the benefit could be subject to a mandatory adjustment for inflation. The projected benefit, after accounting for inflation, could also be reflected in a lump-sum distribution upon separation from service which, under the rule suggested above, would have to be made to an Individual Retirement Account. One way to approximate the required contribution without making an estimate of future inflation is to determine the present value of future benefits based on the expected real rate of return (interest in excess of inflation) rather than the nominal rate of interest, as is now permitted. If actual earnings reflect the real return plus inflation, the balance in the IRA would be sufficient to provide a benefit based upon the employee's earnings at separation of service as adjusted for inflation.

It is not possible, however, to impose additional restrictions on defined-benefit plans, or even to recommend continuation of the present conditions, without consideration of whether employers would be willing to assume the risks imposed by these requirements.

Employer Objections to Defined-Benefit Plans. Defined-benefit plans may be unattractive because of the certainty of greater administrative costs in addition to the cost of benefits or because the actual obligation under such plans is less certain than it would be in the case of a defined-contribution plan.

Administrative costs, particularly actuarial services, may deter some employers, primarily small employers.[97] This may be unavoidable, but the possibility of government assistance deserves more consideration. The PBGC premium is often mentioned as an additional deterrent, but viewed per employee,

---

[97] *The First Decade*, p. 111. Similarly, see *ERISA 10th Anniversary Conference*, p. 47. (Statement of L. Margel.)

and not in the aggregate for a plan, it seems too small to make a significant difference.

In addition to potential liability for past service, discussed in the next part, defined-benefit plans may be more expensive than anticipated if investment return is low, salaries rise faster than estimated, employees retire earlier than anticipated, more employees than expected stay long enough to vest, or Social Security benefits are lower than the assumed level. I have not seen these factors discussed individually. It seems possible to me that if we do so, we either may determine that the problem is not substantial or begin to think seriously of ways to mitigate employers' concerns.

Employers presumably are used to investment risk, and they can enjoy the gains when performance is better than anticipated. Employers unwilling to take this risk should be able to acquire relatively stable fixed-income securities.

It seems likely that real salary growth over a career (i.e., changes that occur in the absence of inflation) can be estimated with reasonable accuracy. If not, salary could be averaged over a somewhat longer period to minimize the risk. Salary changes caused by inflation may be a different matter; these increase costs unless accompanied by a corresponding increase in the market return. An employer's willingness to accept this risk may depend upon the likelihood that inflation will be accompanied by an increase in nominal earnings.[98] Of course, even if this were believed to be fairly likely, it would not help an employer who opted to avoid investment risk through the purchase of fixed-income securities. This suggests that the viability of defined-benefit plans may depend upon the availability of indexed bonds issued by the Treasury. Such an option should certainly be considered.

The required contributions to a defined-benefit plan will also vary with turnover, which is the rate at which employment terminates (including by death or disability) before benefits vest. While this may not impact upon a large group it could conceivably increase the costs of a small employer. This uncertainty,

---

[98]During the 1970s, inflation soared while the market value of investments declined, thereby causing many employers to abandon their defined-benefit plans. *The First Decade*, p. 146.

however, cannot necessarily be avoided by establishment of a defined-contribution plan. If amounts associated with those who leave prior to vesting are used to reduce future employer contributions, the employer cannot be sure of the level of required contributions. The employer does know the maximum amount required, assuming no forfeitures, but this could be determined for a defined-benefit plan as well. In fact, this is the practice when individual insurance contracts are used.

Defined-benefit plans could have an unanticipated increase in costs if they provide for unreduced benefits in the event of early retirement and the number of such retirements exceeds the estimate. It would seem illogical to turn to defined-contribution plans for this reason, however. It would be more sensible to provide actuarially equivalent benefits from defined-benefit plans. If this does not adequately provide for those forced to separate early, neither will a defined-contribution plan. A discussion of the proper treatment of early retirees under private plans, as well as Social Security, is beyond the scope of this chapter.

In sum, it seems to me that uncertainty as to costs need not present substantial barriers to the adoption of defined-benefit plans. If I am right, the principal problem is the potential liability for benefits for service prior to plan establishment which would occur upon an unexpected early termination. I now turn to that question.

Guarantee of Benefits

If investment returns, turnover, and changes in salary are accurately estimated, a terminated defined-benefit plan would generally have sufficient funds to pay accrued benefits except to the extent the employer had not yet funded benefits accrued prior to the establishment of the plan or the adoption of a liberalizing amendment.

There is no obvious way to allocate the burden of such a shortage of funds. If the promised benefit is not paid, the employee is harmed. Similar to the case of vesting, noted above, there is no logical way for the employee to plan for such a risk. To save as if benefits will not be paid does not seem sensible even if it were practical. If the PBGC bore the full burden of terminated plans regardless of the employer's solvency, it would be very difficult to prevent abuse of the system. If employers bore the full burden, they could avoid it by refusing to establish plans.

There are problems with any choice, and present law uneasily allocates the burden among all three.[99] Employers are liable for guaranteed benefits up to 30 percent of net worth.[100] The PBGC assumes the residue when the net worth limit applies.[101] The employee is not fully protected, however, because of the maximum limit on guaranteed benefits and a five-year phasein of the guarantee following a new plan or amendment.[102]

A longer phasein of past service benefits consistent with the practice under a target-benefit plan is one approach worth considering. Under a target-benefit plan, the employer assumes the burden of past service ratably over the projected future career of the employee. If the plan is terminated before the employee reaches retirement age (or if the employee departs before then), the employee receives less than promised. This approach, which also in effect applies to defined-benefit plans funded through individual insurance contracts,[103] can be contrasted with the five-year phasein for most defined-benefit plans.

For example, assume an employee began work at age 35 and had 15 years of service when the plan was adopted. If the plan provides a benefit of 1 percent of pay per year of service, a 30 percent benefit will be projected at retirement at age 65. Under a target-benefit plan, contributions will be made over a 15-year period equal to the amount necessary, with the estimated investment return, to fund the promised benefit. If the plan terminates after five years, it is obvious there will be insufficient funds, even if investments lived up to expectations to provide the 20 percent benefit "accrued" to date. Yet neither the PBGC or the employer is required to make up the difference.

This can be contrasted with a traditional defined-benefit plan. At its inception, such a plan similarly does not have as-

---

[99]Halperin, *Retirement Security*, p. 772.

[100]ERISA Section 4062(b), 29 U.S.C. Section 1361(b).

[101]ERISA Section 4061, 29 U.S.C. Section 1361.

[102]ERISA Section 4022(b), 29 U.S.C. Section 1322(b).

[103]IRC Section 411(b)(1)(F), 412(i). See Halperin, *Retirement Security*, p. 777.

sets to pay past service benefits and funding is generally spread over a 30-year period. If the plan terminates with insufficient assets to pay vested benefits, however, the PBGC will make up the shortage subject to its right to reimbursement from the employer up to 30 percent of the employer's net worth. In this case, subject to the maximum limit on insured benefits, the 20 percent accrued benefit will be paid. Is this essential?

The employee had no expectation before the plan was established. Would it be reasonable to phase in the right to past service benefits more slowly? Would this have a significant impact on adoption of defined-benefit plans? This is a complex question, but I believe it clearly desirable to make the regulatory burden on defined-contribution and defined-benefit plans more equal. If we maintain the incentive for defined-benefit plans and the calculation of vested benefits under such plans is adjusted to reflect potential postseparation increases in earnings, we should have more retirement security than we would if the trend toward defined-contribution plans accelerates.

Can Employer Plans Do the Job?

We have considered above the possibility of increasing the coverage of existing plans and improving the chances they will actually provide replacement income. But many employers have not established qualified plans, and it is at least possible that some employers who now have such plans will not continue to maintain them if coverage must be increased. It is essential to consider, therefore, whether present tax incentives should be continued as well as potential alternatives.

Nonqualified Plans

One possible deterrent to the establishment of qualified plans is the availability of so-called nonqualified retirement arrangements limited to highly paid employees. The tax incentive for qualified plans is ineffective if the highly paid employee can obtain virtually the same benefit from nonqualified deferred-compensation arrangements without being subject to the nondiscrimination test. Unfortunately, this is often possible under present law.

Qualified plans provide two benefits. First, tax is deferred until receipt of a pension, which usually occurs after retirement when marginal rates may be reduced. Second, earnings of the plan are not taxed. The first of these advantages—deferral—is available with nonqualified compensation as long as the employee is willing to rely on the credit of the employer and forgo separate funding.[104] Further, if marginal rates are not reduced, deferral is not a permanent advantage since the tax paid on the larger deferred distribution is equivalent in present value terms to the tax that is deferred.[105] The real benefit—the tax exemption for earnings—is intended to be limited to qualified plans. However, since amounts set aside can be considered part of the employer's assets, tax-free investment income clearly is available if the employer is a government or a tax-exempt institution. A similar advantage exists in the case of a nominally taxable employer if it has unused tax losses or if the income is in the form of dividends[106] or the investment[107] is in employer stock.

In the case of employees of tax-exempt charitable institutions or public schools, both deferral and tax-sheltered buildup can be obtained, despite separate funding, by making use of so-called tax-sheltered annuities (TSAs).[108] My impression is that many of these institutions (colleges and universities) provide better retirement benefits for the higher-paid employees (faculty and administrators) than they do for lower-paid employees (clerical and maintenance).

In 1978, Congress imposed a limitation on the deferral of nonqualified compensation for employees of government.[109] The President recommends a similar limitation for employees

---

[104]Rev. Rul. 60-31, 1960–1 C.B. 174.

[105]Halperin, *Interest in Disguise*, p. 522.

[106]Under I.R.C. Section 243, a corporation can deduct 85 percent of dividends received.

[107]Under I.R.C. Section 1032, a corporation does not pay tax on appreciation in its own securities. See Halperin, *Interest in Disguise*, p. 540.

[108]I.R.C. Section 403(b).

[109]I.R.C. Section 457.

of tax-exempt institutions.[110] It may be preferable to allow deferral of even nonqualified deferred compensation, but to impose a special tax on the investment income earned on deferred amounts at the rate that would be paid by the employee rather than the employer.[111] This denies the advantage—a lower tax burden on investment income—intended to be achieved by the deferral of income. In addition, tax-sheltered annuities should be eliminated so that charitable institutions would have to rely on qualified plans to provide funded deferred compensation on a tax-preferred basis.

When Are Qualified Plans Desired by Employers?

Many employers try to avoid coverage of low- and moderate-income employees; they do whatever they can to avoid the intent of the nondiscrimination test. It is therefore claimed that more required coverage will mean fewer plans. However, most people believe that the cost of the pension plan is reflected in lower wages. If employees bear the cost of pensions, why should employers worry about coverage?

It may be that low- and moderate-income employees do not value pensions as much as current wages. They would prefer to work for companies without pension plans or at least they will not accept a wage cut equal to the cost of the pension plan. There are a number of possible reasons for this behavior.

Since pensions may not be vested, an employee may be asked to give up, for example, $100 in current wages in return for a 10 percent chance for a pension with a present value of $1,000. Many would not accept the gamble. If this is the operative possibility, then faster vesting would make pensions more acceptable and reduce the cost of the program in the sense that more of the cost could be passed on to lower earning employees.

It is also possible that some employees have a short time horizon. They are not thinking of retirement. For these people even a fully vested pension with a present value of $1,000 may be treated as practically worthless. Finally, it may be perfectly

---

[110] *The President's Tax Proposals*, chap. 14.10.

[111] See Halperin, *Interest in Disguise*, pp. 544–50, for development of this recommendation.

rational for an employee to consider it to be the wrong time to save for retirement. Given other pressing needs of the moment, retirement savings should come later.

If an employer cannot pass along the full cost of the pension benefit to the low- and moderate-income employee, it must look to another source. It is unlikely that the cost can be passed along to customers. There is little reason to expect it to come out of profits, unless profits substantially increase due to reduced turnover or more satisfied employees. The likely source is the compensation paid to the higher-income employees.

Higher-income employees obtain substantial tax benefits by saving through a qualified plan. Assuming they desire to save, the adoption of a qualified plan effectively increases their earnings. Since the existence of such plan ultimately depends on satisfying the wage demands of the lower paid, the highly paid may have to relinquish part of their tax savings to increase the compensation of the low earner. If they can do so and still come out ahead, the qualified plan is desirable. This scenario explains efforts to avoid the antidiscrimination test and the argument that a maximum limitation on benefits will cause curtailment of plans. As the participation of the lower paid increases, the cost, in terms of higher overall wages, to compensate them for the fact that they receive part of their earnings in the form of "valueless" pensions, similarly increases. At the same time, if the benefits of the higher paid are reduced, there is less to use for such compensation. The point may be reached where the amount required to pacify the lower income exceeds the tax savings. When this occurs, however, will vary from employer to employer, depending upon the makeup of the work force and their interest in retirement income.[112]

This description illustrates the difficulty of the voluntary approach to meeting the goals of public policy. A government subsidy, through tax relief or otherwise, may help direct private behavior, but the more stringent the conditions for obtaining the subsidy, the less likely it becomes that employers will respond. It is essential to consider not only the ultimate aim but whether too great a push toward that aim could be counterproductive.

---

[112]Wolk, *Discrimination Rules*, pp. 430–33.

There is no easy answer to this dilemma. Obviously, it is not worthwhile to provide huge tax savings to a highly paid owner in the hope he might provide a few crumbs to his employees. More of this was allowed to occur prior to ERISA, and I see no reason to turn back the clock. Qualified plans should be required to provide substantial benefits to rank and file employees and should be limited in the amount and possibly the proportion that can go to the highly paid. If this is insufficient to provide adequate retirement security for low- and moderate-income employees, it is time to consider another approach.

Alternatives to Qualified Plans

It is reasonable to believe that a significant part of the work force will never be adequately covered by employer retirement programs as presently conceived. No more than 70 percent of full-time workers over 25 are covered today.[113] No one seems to be predicting coverage for more than 70 percent of retirees even among those who are now just starting their careers.[114] Employees without coverage will be heavily concentrated among lower-paid employees for whom individual savings are impractical.[115] It is hard to justify an increase in the tax burden on this group in order to help provide for the retirement income of the more highly paid when the retirement income of the former will fall short of the need.

If full replacement of preretirement income is a goal, it is necessary to consider other alternatives. Some would recommend expansion of Social Security to more nearly approximate full replacement.[116] Others, including the president's commission, have suggested that all employers be required to provide a minimum level of fully vested retirement benefits for all employees.[117]

---

[113] *1985 Hearings on Retirement Income Security*. (Statement of the Chamber of Commerce of the United States.)

[114] *The First Decade*, p. 121.

[115] *ERISA 10th Anniversary Conference*, p. 42. (Statement of D. Grubbs.)

[116] Bernstein, "Mandatory Pension Coverage: An Idea Whose Time Is Past." (Paper presented to the President's Commission on Pension Policy, April 17, 1980.)

[117] *Coming of Age*, p. 42; Grubbs, "An Adequate Retirement Income for Every American," *Employee Benefits Journal* 26 (Winter 1980).

Both of these approaches are more promising than potential expansion of the voluntary private system, but neither seems politically viable at the present time. If revenue is the obstacle, it may be argued that repeal of the favorable tax treatment for qualified plans and IRAs could raise the funds needed to provide additional Social Security benefits.[118] However, it appears likely that expansion of the tax base will have to be coupled with rate reduction rather than additional expenditures.

Others may look to the private system to do the job. Either they are satisfied that incomplete coverage is the best we can do or they hold some hope for additional coverage. The latter seems unlikely unless we somehow manage to increase interest in retirement protection among the lower paid or can develop new approaches that tailor the tax subsidy to the amount essential to secure coverage of the lower income without an additional windfall for the higher paid. We may lack the tools to do this or the will to provide greater benefits only to those employers who would not otherwise have plans. Perhaps we need to think about the possibility of providing additional tax benefits for contributions on behalf of certain income groups to plans which provide an unusually large proportion of their benefits for this group.

At this point no viable means of increasing coverage seems on the horizon. Perhaps none ever will appear, but it would certainly help if we were able to develop a consensus that such coverage is so essential that the best approach, no matter how imperfect, should be tried. On the other hand, if there is a general consensus that certain means just will not do, it would again help if its supporters recognized this and began to explore other avenues. At the moment, I would hope that such discussion and exploration would increase the support for mandatory pension arrangements, perhaps aided by additional tax subsidies for specified contributions. Perhaps by the 21st century this will occur.

---

[118]The estimated revenue loss for 1985 is over $67 billion.